75 Easy Life Science
Demonstrations

Thomas Kardos
illustrated by Nicholas Soloway

J. WESTON

WALCH
PUBLISHER
Portland, Maine

Dedication

This book is dedicated to my darling wife, Pearl, who throughout this project assisted me with great patience. As a nonscience educator, she helped me develop this book into an easy-to-use and comprehensible resource.

1   2   3   4   5   6   7   8   9   10

ISBN 0-8251-2854-4

Copyright © 1996
J. Weston Walch, Publisher
P. O. Box 658 • Portland, Maine 04104-0658

Printed in the United States of America

Contents

Preface . . . . *vii*

   My Philosophy of Education . . . . *viii*

Suggestions for Teachers . . . . *ix*

   Equipment . . . . *x*

   Safety Procedures . . . . *xi*

1. STIMULUS AND RESPONSE 1
2. GRAVITROPISM (GEOTROPISM) 2
3. PHOTOTROPISM #1: PLANTS GROW TOWARD LIGHT 3
4. PHOTOTROPISM #2: GROWING VEGETABLE TOPS 4
5. WATER IS NEEDED BY ALL LIVING ORGANISMS 5
6. AIR IS IMPORTANT 5
7. HUMANS EXHALE CARBON DIOXIDE #1 6
8. HUMANS EXHALE CARBON DIOXIDE #2 7
9. TESTING FOR CARBON DIOXIDE 8
10. TESTING THE GASES PLANTS EMIT 8
11. YEAST AND CARBON DIOXIDE 9
12. THE GREENHOUSE EFFECT 10
13. STOMATA IN PLANTS 11
14. TRANSPIRATION—PLANT WATER LOSS 12
15. PLANTS GIVE OUT WATER (VAPOR) 12
16. LEAF SKELETONS 13
17. SEED GROWTH VARIABLES 14
18. HUMANS EXHALE WATER VAPOR 15
19. LEAF SHAPE AND WATER EVAPORATION IN PLANTS 16
20. ANIMALS EXHALE CARBON DIOXIDE 17
21. CARBON DIOXIDE-OXYGEN CYCLE 18
22. ANIMAL CIRCULATION 19
23. PLANTS HAVE CIRCULATION (CAPILLARITY) 20
24. CELL MODEL USING GELATIN 21
25. TESTING FOR STARCH IN FOODS 21
26. TESTING FOR SUGAR IN FOODS 22
27. TESTING FOR MINERALS IN FOODS 23

28. TESTING FOR FATS IN FOODS 23
29. TESTING FOR PROTEIN IN FOODS #1 24
30. TESTING FOR PROTEIN IN FOODS #2 25
31. TESTING FOR VITAMIN C IN FOODS 26
32. TESTING FOR WATER IN FOODS .26
33. TESTING FOR SALT 27
34. CHLOROPHYLL AND CHROMATOGRAPHY 27
35. BIODEGRADABLE MATERIALS 28
36. VITAMINS: THEIR IMPORTANCE TO US 29
37. MINERALS: THEIR IMPORTANCE TO US 30
38. SEPARATING OUT IRON FROM CREAM OF WHEAT 31
39. PERISTALSIS 31
40. MECHANICAL DIGESTION 32
41. CHEMICAL DIGESTION 32
42. PREDIGESTING FOOD IN THE MOUTH 33
43. DIGESTION 34
44. STOMACH CHEMISTRY: PEPSIN AND HYDROCHLORIC ACID 35
45. HEAT AIDS DIGESTION 36
46. BILE: AN EMULSIFIER FOR FATS 37
47. MODEL OF THE SMALL INTESTINE 38
48. THE HEARTBEAT AND PULSE 39
49. NICOTINE SPEEDS UP HEARTBEAT 40
50. NICOTINE AND LIVING THINGS 41
51. INDOOR PLANT INFESTATION: NICOTINE SPRAY FOR PLANTS 42
52. BIOLOGICAL CONTROL OF PESTS 43
53. ASTHMA AND EMPHYSEMA 44
54. KEEPING COOL 45
55. REDI'S EXPERIMENT: SOURCE OF LIVING THINGS 45
56. ASEXUAL REPRODUCTION: BUDDING (YEAST CELLS AND BREAD) . . .46
57. ASEXUAL REPRODUCTION: SPORULATION (SPORES AND MOLDS) . . 47
58. ASEXUAL REPRODUCTION: VEGETATIVE PROPAGATION 47
59. SEXUAL REPRODUCTION 48
60. INSECT MULTIPLICATION: FRUIT FLIES 48
61. INSECT MULTIPLICATION: GENERATIONS 49
62. INHERITED TRAITS 50
63. ENVIRONMENT AFFECTS EXPRESSION OF GENES 50
64. FISH AND COLOR 51
65. VARIABLES AFFECT HABITAT 52
66. EARTHWORMS 53
67. THE LIFE OF EARTHWORMS 54
68. METAMORPHOSIS 55

69. SOUNDS PEOPLE HEAR 56
70. HOW MUCH SOIL PLANTS USE 57
71. HYDROPONICS 58
72. MOLDS 60
73. REDUCING SOIL EROSION WITH PLANTS 60
74. DIFFUSION 62
75. TESTING GROWING ROOTS FOR ACID 63

Appendix 65
   DENSITY OF LIQUIDS 66
   ALTITUDE, BAROMETER, AND BOILING POINT 66
   SPECIFIC GRAVITY 66
   CONVERSION OF TEMPERATURE:
     CELSIUS TO FAHRENHEIT 67
   CONVERSION OF TEMPERATURE:
     FAHRENHEIT TO CELSIUS 68

Glossary 69

Index 73

Preface

As a middle school teacher, many times I found myself wishing for a quick and easy demonstration to illustrate a word, a concept, or a principle in science. Also I often wanted a brief explanation to conveniently review basics and additional facts without looking through many texts.

This book is a collection of many classroom demonstrations. Explanation is provided so that you can quickly review key concepts. Basic scientific ideas are hard to present on a concrete level; this book fills that specific need. Some of the demonstrations could be repeated as classroom activities. A few require more time than just one class period.

The actual teacher demonstration is something full of joy and expectation, like a thriller with an unexpected twist ending. Keep it that way and enjoy it! Try everything beforehand.

We need to support each other and leave footprints in the sands of time. Teaching is a living art. Happy journey! Happy sciencing!

—Thomas Kardos

MY PHILOSOPHY OF EDUCATION

My personal philosophy of education involves many themes:

1. Students must feel like participants in the joy of sciencing.

2. Students need many hands-on experiences. Invite them to experiment at home. This invitation must be limited by the availability of equipment and the relative safety of the activity. Many experiments can be done with informal equipment such as recycled jars, soda cans, and bottles. Inexpensive plastic measuring cups can replace graduated cylinders.

3. Students need to form in their own minds a concept of what science is. Do not encourage rote memorization. Science is a series of stories that need the participant's intervention. Let your students jump in and get involved in these stories.

4. Teachers do not have to answer all student questions. It is wonderful to let your students know that you are a limited resource. Let students go out and find some difficult answers. Maybe there are none. Nobody on this planet has all the answers. It is important that you teach your students the concept that humans have limits, but these can change. Let students know that through networking (cooperative effort) they, too, can find some of the harder answers.

5. People are concrete operators. Their learning starts with real objects and lots of manipulations and eventually ends in abstract reasoning and concept formation. This is why people draw sketches for you, to explain their ideas. Read summaries or explanations of Piaget's learning theory; it will change your teaching style for life.

6. Be open to change. Be prepared to change as you progress in teaching. The world around us changes and so must our teaching style.

7. Finally, realize that you cannot do it all. Your many science students become your followers. You will start a science revolution! This is your real opportunity!

Suggestions for Teachers

1. A • (bullet) denotes a demonstration. Several headings have multiple demonstrations.

2. MATERIALS: Provides an accurate list of materials needed. You can make substitutions and changes, as you find appropriate.

3. Since many demonstrations are small and are not clearly visible from the back of the room, you will need to take this into account as part of your classroom-management technique. Students need to see the entire procedure, step by step.

4. Some demonstrations require that students make observations over a short period of time. It is important that they observe the changes in progress. One choice is to videotape the event and replay it several times.

5. Some demonstrations can be enhanced by bottom illumination: Place the demonstration on the overhead projector and lower the mirror so that no image is projected overhead.

6. Encourage students to repeat certain carefully selected demonstrations in class or at home.

7. Key words are included in the Index for easier access to the demonstrations.

8. I use a 30-cup coffeepot to heat water for student experiments and to perform many demonstrations in lieu of an electric hot plate, pans, and more cumbersome equipment.

9. I may use temperature Fahrenheit in some places, since most younger students relate to it better.

10. A few demonstrations may appear difficult to set up, for they have many parts. Be patient, follow the listing's steps, and you will really succeed with them.

EQUIPMENT

- Sometimes, though rarely, I will call for equipment that you may not have. An increasing growth in technology tends to complicate matters. Skip these few demonstrations or borrow the equipment from your local high school teacher. Review with him or her the proper and safe use of the equipment. These special demonstrations will add immensely to your power as an effective educator and will enhance your professionalism.

- Try all demonstrations in advance to smooth your show. If something fails, enjoy it and teach with it. Many great science discoveries had to be done over many times before their first success. Dr. Land had to do more than 11,000 experiments to develop the instant color photograph. Most people would have quit long before that.

- One of my favorite techniques is to use a camcorder and show the demonstration on a large monitor.

SAFETY PROCEDURES

- Follow all local, state, and federal safety procedures: Protect your students and yourself from harm.

- Wear required safety equipment when handling hazardous materials, such as laboratory acids or anything stronger than ordinary vinegar.

- Label all containers and use original containers.

- Attend safety classes to be up-to-date on the latest classroom safety procedures. Much new legislation has been adopted in the recent past.

- Have evacuation plans clearly posted, planned, and actually tested.

- Dispose of demonstration materials in a safe way. Obtain your district's guidelines on this matter.

- Have an ABC-rated fire extinguisher on hand at all times. Use a Halon™ gas extinguisher for electronic equipment.

- Learn how to use a fire extinguisher properly.

- Neutralize all acids and bases prior to disposal.

- Have students wash their hands whenever they come into contact with anything that may be remotely harmful to them, even if years later, like lead.

- Conduct demonstrations at a distance so that no one is harmed should anything go wrong.

- Practice your demonstration if it is totally new to you. A few demonstrations do require some prior practice.

DISCLAIMER

These safety rules are provided only as a guide. They are neither complete nor totally inclusive. The publisher and the author do not assume any responsibility for actions or consequences in following instructions provided in this demonstration book.

1. STIMULUS AND RESPONSE

When living things act or make a change, it is in **response** to some change in their environment—a **stimulus**. A stimulus can be heat, light, sound, electric energy, etc. Animals respond quickly to stimuli, while plants respond slowly and in many different ways.

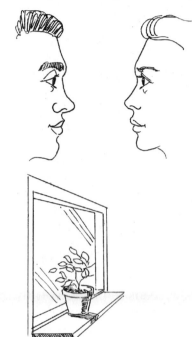

- Ask all students to pair off. They should sit facing each other, about six inches apart, and look at each other's eyes. Turn off the room lights. Wait about 15–20 seconds, then turn the lights on (stimulus). Students should immediately notice the change in the pupils of their eyes (response), due to the sudden change in light.

- Take a plant and turn it so that its leaves face away from a window. In a few days, students should notice that the leaves turn toward the window light.

2. GRAVITROPISM (GEOTROPISM)

Plants actually move during growth in response to certain environmental stimuli. Auxins, growth hormones produced in the tips of stems and roots, are responsible for growth movements in plants called **tropism**.

Sensitivity to gravity is called **gravitropism**, or **geotropism**. In this activity, you will observe the effect of gravity on plant growth.

Chemotropism is plant growth movement in response to chemicals. **Heliotropism** is movement toward or away from sunlight. **Phototropism** is the movement of the plant toward or away from light. **Hydrotropism** is movement in response to water. **Thigmotropism** is a movement in response to touch.

MATERIALS: corn seeds, empty glass jar with lid, layer of nonabsorbent cotton, paper towels, small amount of clay, water

- Soak the corn seed in water for a couple of days. Arrange the seeds evenly on the bottom of the jar with the pointed ends facing inward. Place a layer of nonabsorbent cotton over them, then fill the jar with paper towels to hold the cotton and the seeds in place. Wet the paper towels thoroughly and place the lid securely on the jar. Place the jar on its side, so that one seed points up; you can use a few pieces of clay along the side of the jar to keep it from rolling. Place the jar in a dim light. Make observations through the bottom of the jar over a five- to seven-day period.

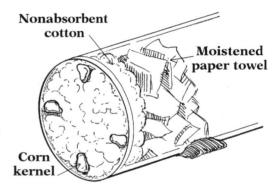

3. PHOTOTROPISM #1: PLANTS GROW TOWARD LIGHT

Phototropism is the movement of plants toward or away from light.

MATERIALS: three or four plastic sandwich bags, three or four paper towels, four or five beans (different kinds are fine) per bag, water, tacks or staples

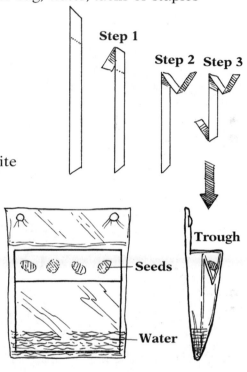

- If the paper towel is wider than the sandwich bag, cut it so it is slightly narrower than the bag width.

  Step 1. Prepare a trough by folding the paper towel one inch from the upper edge.

  Step 2. Make another fold an inch below the first one, but in the opposite direction; viewed from the side, the folds should look like the letter N.

  Step 3. Fold back the lower end of the paper towel so that the trough assembly will fit inside the bag. Place four or five bean seeds in the trough. Attach the plastic bag to a wall or bulletin board with tacks or staples. Fill the bottom of the bag with about one-half inch of water; water it every few days. If you start the activity on a Thursday or Friday, you will have germination by Monday. The plants that grow will have exaggerated stalks pointing toward the room lights or windows. Plant several bags with seeds in different locations of your room to demonstrate plant growth toward light.

4. PHOTOTROPISM #2: GROWING VEGETABLE TOPS

Many vegetables can grow in midair and even upside down. They will grow in the direction of light sources. This is **phototropism**.

MATERIALS: paring knife, large carrot, small plate, paper towels, wooden toothpick, cotton thread or string, water

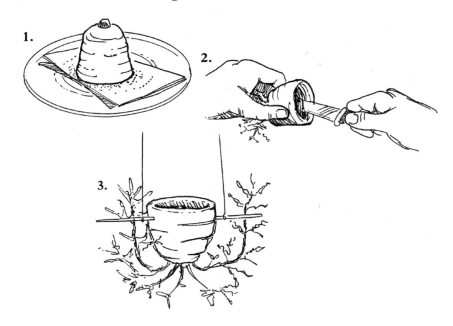

- Use the paring knife to cut a two- or three-inch section from the top of the carrot. (Be sure to cut away from your body.) Leave any shoots or stalk attached to the carrot. Place the cut end on the plate over some moist paper towels. Keep the paper moist and keep the plate in sunlight. Once shoots begin to grow out of the carrot, remove the carrot and hollow out its cut side with the pairing knife. Poke a toothpick through it and use the toothpick ends and string or thread to hang the plant in a sunny location. Fill the carrot cavity with water and keep it wet at all times. More shoots will sprout from the carrot and they will all point upward and toward the light.

5. WATER IS NEEDED BY ALL LIVING ORGANISMS

MATERIALS: two jars with lids, stale bread, water, dirt, crayon

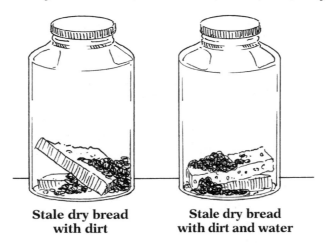

Stale dry bread with dirt   **Stale dry bread with dirt and water**

- Place some stale, dry bread in each jar, and sprinkle it with dirt. Sprinkle a few drops of water on one sample and mark this jar with a large crayon mark. Close both jars and place them in a warm place for several days. Notice the growth of mold on the bread that was wet. It will have gray or greenish spots.

6. AIR IS IMPORTANT

Most plants and animals can go for days without food or water, but they die in just minutes without air. Air is important; it is a mixture of gases, and one fifth of it is **oxygen**, which is essential for animal life. Most organisms (aerobic organisms) get their oxygen from air or water. Anaerobic organisms get it from compounds of oxygen.

MATERIALS: glass tumbler, water

- Fill a glass nearly full of water and let it stand overnight. The next day, students should notice the bubbles on the inside walls of the glass. These are air bubbles, coming from the air that is dissolved in water. The bubbles contain oxygen.

Air bubbles

7. HUMANS EXHALE CARBON DIOXIDE #1

Oxidation is the rapid process during which fuels combine with oxygen, giving off heat. Humans get their energy from foods, and oxidize mainly sugar. The process, slow in humans, is described as slow oxidation. Humans inhale air, which is about 20% oxygen, and exhale **carbon dioxide**, a smaller amount of oxygen, water, and other gases. Limewater is a colorless liquid. In the presence of carbon dioxide, it turns milky or cloudy. Limewater is used as an indicator; it changes its physical appearance when it reacts with a specific substance. The change is usually in color or turbidity. It is sufficiently large that an untrained person will notice the change.

MATERIALS: limewater, glass, drinking straw

Limewater

- Fill the glass about half-full of limewater and start bubbling air through it with the straw. In a short time, the limewater will turn milky white. This shows the presence of carbon dioxide.

8. HUMANS EXHALE CARBON DIOXIDE #2

Humans inhale oxygen and exhale carbon dioxide, water vapor, and small amounts of oxygen. Bromthymol blue is blue in the presence of bases, pale green when neutral, and yellow(ish) with acids.

MATERIALS: small glass or beaker, drinking straw, bromthymol blue, water

| Blue | Greenish | Yellowish |

- Place a drop of bromthymol blue in half a glass of water and bubble air through it. The bluish water will appear to become paler, first greenish, then yellowish. The carbon dioxide in your breath mixed with water to form carbonic acid and bromthymol blue reacted to show the presence of an acid.

9. TESTING FOR CARBON DIOXIDE

Plants, like animals, have **respiration**. Their respiration waste includes carbon dioxide and water vapor.

MATERIALS: small leafy plant, large jar with lid (big enough to contain the plant), small container (baby food jar), limewater

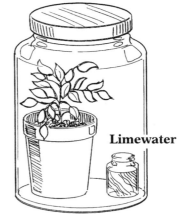

- Place the plant inside the large jar. Fill the small container with limewater and place it inside the jar. Close the jar and store it in a dark place overnight. Notice how the limewater turns cloudy.

Limewater

10. TESTING THE GASES PLANTS EMIT

During the process of respiration, plants in the dark emit carbon dioxide. Plants in the light emit oxygen as a by-product of **photosynthesis**. Oxygen is a key component of fire, while carbon dioxide puts out fires.

MATERIALS: two sprigs of elodea or other water plant, two test tubes, water, two wide-mouthed jars, matches or lit candle

- Place a sprig of elodea into each of two test tubes full of water. Make certain that the two sprigs are of equal length. Place a couple of inches of water in each. Place your finger over one test tube, so that you do not lose any water, invert it, and place it inside one jar. Repeat with the other test tube. Now you have two identical setups. Place one in a dark closet, the other in the sun or under a grow lamp. After a couple of days, some

In the dark   **In the light**

gas should have collected at the upper end of the test tubes. Carefully invert each test tube, keeping it closed with your finger. Holding a burning match or candle near each test tube, let the gas escape. The gas from one test tube will glow brightly, while the gas from the other might extinguish the flame.

11. YEAST AND CARBON DIOXIDE

Yeast is a tiny living fungus that produces carbon dioxide as part of its reproduction. This makes yeast valuable in the production of bread, wine, and other alcoholic beverages. It can be also used as a dietary supplement, because it is rich in protein. Yeast reproduces by **fission** and **budding**. During fission, the cells divide; during budding, they form a small growth called a bud. During reproduction, yeast produces enzymes that break down sugar. Carbon dioxide is a by-product of this activity. When carbon dioxide is trapped in dough, it creates the air pockets that make bread soft.

MATERIALS: empty one-liter soda bottle, balloon, small funnel, several rubber bands or piece of string, empty glass or plastic jar, teaspoon, five teaspoons sugar, one teaspoon yeast, water, limewater (If you do not have lime-water, stir a teaspoon of garden lime into a jar of water.)

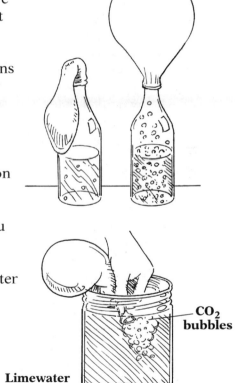

CO$_2$ bubbles

Limewater

- Half-fill jar with warm water and add five teaspoons of sugar. Stir the sugar until it is dissolved. Pour this solution into the soda bottle. Wash the jar and add to it one teaspoon of yeast and three teaspoons of water. Stir well, then add to the sugar solution in the bottle. Attach a deflated balloon to the mouth of the bottle and tie it down tightly with several loops of rubber band or string. Place the bottle in a warm place and observe. The balloon will slowly inflate with carbon dioxide. Fill the jar with limewater. Carefully pinch the neck of the balloon so that you do not lose any gas, and remove it from the jar. Place the pinched end of the balloon below the surface of the limewater and slowly let the gas bubble out and escape. The limewater, a clear liquid, will turn milky, indicating the presence of carbon dioxide.

12. THE GREENHOUSE EFFECT

The **atmosphere** is a thin layer of gases that surround the earth. Among these gases are nitrogen, oxygen, ozone, and carbon dioxide. Since the Industrial Revolution, the amount of carbon dioxide in the atmosphere has been steadily increasing. Infrared rays, the heat energy of the sun, pass easily through the atmosphere. The earth reflects most of the heat back to the sky, but the carbon dioxide in the atmosphere acts as a lid to reflect back and trap some of the heat energy. This has begun a trend in global warming called the **greenhouse effect**. Most nations are starting to address this common problem by trying to reduce their carbon dioxide output. In this activity, you will compare plant growth in an environment that closely duplicates this phenomenon with plant growth in a normal environment.

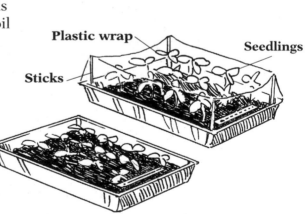

MATERIALS: two seed trays, soil, seeds for flowers, water, plastic food wrap, two thermometers, large rubber band, wooden skewers or ice-cream sticks, pencil, notebook

- In cold climates, do this demonstration in the spring; in warm climates, any season will do. Fill the seed trays with soil, and plant several kinds of flower seeds in them. Make certain that the soil is moist. Place a thermometer in each tray. Cover one tray with plastic wrap, securing it by placing the large rubber band around the tray. Place both trays in an outside location. Shelter them from rain but expose them to the sun. As the seedlings grow taller, insert the ice-cream sticks in the corners of the wrapped tray to keep the plastic from touching the plants, then replace the plastic wrap. Weekly, observe and record the temperatures of both trays. You will notice that the closed environment is warmer than the other tray.

13. STOMATA IN PLANTS

Plants have tiny openings called **stomata** on the underside of their leaves. The function of the stomata is to let out excessive gases, such as oxygen, and to take in carbon dioxide. If the stomata are blocked, the leaf is unable to take in carbon dioxide and dies.

MATERIALS: petroleum jelly, leafy potted plant (geraniums work well)

- Keep the plant in the dark for several days. Then select two leaves and coat their upper surface heavily with petroleum jelly. Select two more leaves and heavily coat their undersurface with petroleum jelly. Place the plant in a sunny window for a week and observe. The leaves coated on the underside will appear to die as time goes on.

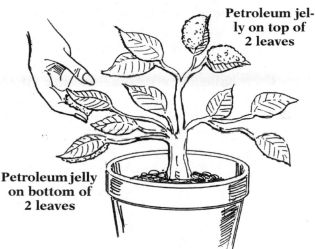

Petroleum jelly on top of 2 leaves

Petroleum jelly on bottom of 2 leaves

14. Transpiration—Plant Water Loss

Plants absorb water from the earth. Water moves up from the roots, through vessels and tracheids, to reach the leaves. Most of the water in the leaves, about 90%, is lost through the stomata. This water loss through the stomata is called **transpiration**. Since large trees can lose as much as 6800 kg (14,900 lb) of water in half a day, this transpiration can affect the local weather (microweather) in terms of humidity and temperature. A plant that runs out of water in the soil will transpire itself to death.

MATERIALS: leafy plant, sandwich bag, sealing tape

• Place the sandwich bag over one leaf of the plant. Use tape to seal the bag tightly around the stem. Place the plant in the sun for several hours. Observe the interior of the bag for cloudiness, as water collects on its inner surface. After several hours in the sun, the bag will show water condensation and will be slightly cloudy.

15. Plants Give Out Water (Vapor)

MATERIALS: small leafy plant, large jar with lid, cobalt chloride indicator paper

Cobalt chloride paper

• Place the plant and a strip of cobalt chloride in the jar. Cover the jar and set it in a dark place overnight. The paper will turn from cobalt blue to pink. The pink indicates the presence of water.

• You can test the cobalt chloride paper by blowing on it. Water vapor in your breath will turn the cobalt chloride pink.

16. LEAF SKELETONS

Leaves and stems are shaped by the woody vessels that conduct water through the plant. These vessels can be compared to the human system of arteries and veins. Holding up a leaf to the light will let you see this woody skeleton. To study it more closely, you can isolate the skeleton and mount it on cardboard. Obtain a variety of leaves from a local park or your garden. Use a tree guidebook to identify the leaves.

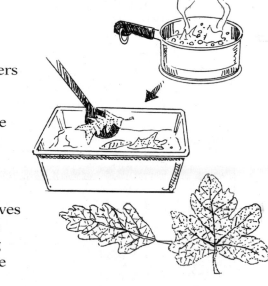

MATERIALS: water, leaves, washing soda, saucepan, plastic tub, slotted spoon, household bleach, paper towels, cardboard, newspapers, rubber gloves, hot plate

- Fill the saucepan about three-quarters full of water. Add one teaspoon of washing soda and bring it to a boil. Add the leaves and boil them for one hour. If you have too many leaves, do it in two batches. In the plastic tub make a solution of water and household bleach, six parts water to one part bleach. Wear rubber gloves and be careful not to spill either the bleach or the bleach solution. Using the slotted spoon, carefully place the boiled leaves in the bleach solution. By next morning, everything but the woody skeletons of the leaves will have floated away. Remove the leaves and arrange them on paper towels (on top of several layers of newspaper) to dry. When the skeletons are dry, they are ready for mounting on cardboard and labeling.

CAUTION! Protect your clothes and work area from the bleach. Immediately wash anything that gets splashed with bleach or bleach solution. If your skin comes in contact with bleach or bleach solution, rinse the affected area under running water.

17. SEED GROWTH VARIABLES

Seeds germinate and grow under specific conditions. Different varieties of seeds may do best under different conditions. This activity will address four variables: warmth, light, water, and air. It is important to note that when you test for one variable, the other three must be kept unchanged. Corn or beans are good choices for this demonstration, as they germinate quickly. You will use two dishes: one to experiment with, the other as a control. The results of this activity will show that seeds need sufficient water, warm temperatures, oxygen, and sunlight to germinate and grow.

MATERIALS: eight small dishes, corn or bean seeds, wax pencil or water-proof felt pen, baking pan, ice cubes, blotting paper or cotton, small piece of glass (as from picture frame), water

- Place a piece of blotter paper or a thin layer of cotton in each of the eight small dishes. Number each one. Place ten or twelve seeds of the same variety on top of the blotter or cotton in every dish. Then expose each dish to the conditions described in the table:

DISH #	CONDITION 1	CONDITION 2
1	water	keep next to #2 on a table
2	do not water	keep next to #1 on a table
3	water	set in warm place
4	water	keep in pan over ice cubes
5	water	place in sunny window
6	water	place in dark closet
7	water	cover with glass (blocks air)
8	water	leave exposed to air

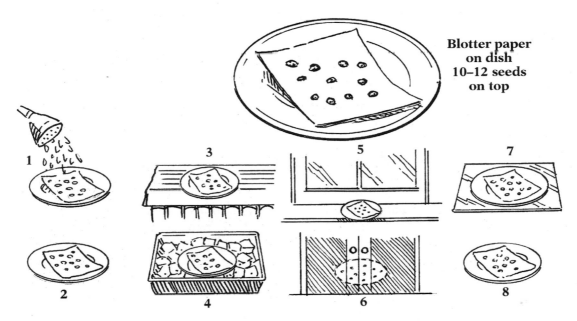

Blotter paper
on dish
10–12 seeds
on top

After several days, observe the results in each dish. Plants in a warm dish will grow better than plants on ice. Seeds in the dark may germinate better than those in the light, as light is not needed for germination. It is dark in the ground where seeds are planted. Seeds left without either air or water will not germinate.

18. HUMANS EXHALE WATER VAPOR

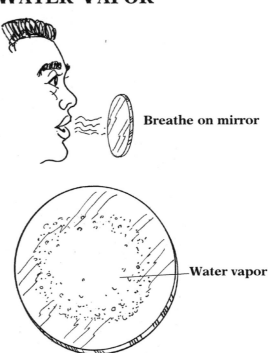

Humans inhale air, which is a mixture of oxygen and other gases—mostly nitrogen. We exhale water vapor, nitrogen, a smaller amount of oxygen, carbon dioxide, and other trace gases.

MATERIALS: small mirror

- Breathe on a mirror to show that you are producing water vapor. Your breath will condense, leaving a haze of moisture on the glass.

Breathe on mirror

Water vapor

19. LEAF SHAPE AND WATER EVAPORATION IN PLANTS

The shape of a leaf determines how quickly water will evaporate from it. On a broad leaf with a larger surface area, water will evaporate faster than on a narrow one with a smaller surface area. The speed at which water evaporates is called the **evaporation rate**. Desert plants have leaves that are thick and round with a greatly reduced surface area. They are also waxy, which inhibits evaporation. This explains why desert plants have a very slow rate of water evaporation.

MATERIALS: four paper towels, wax paper, paper clips, water

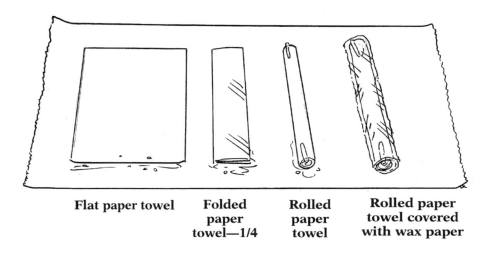

**Flat paper towel   Folded   Rolled   Rolled paper
                        paper   paper   towel covered
                        towel—1/4   towel   with wax paper**

- Dampen all paper towels equally so that they are wet but do not drip. Lay one towel flat on a piece of wax paper, two or three feet long. Fold the next sheet in half, then in half again, and place on the wax paper next to the first towel but not touching it. Roll up the third and fasten the ends with two paper clips, then place it on the wax paper. Finally, place the last towel on a piece of wax paper the same size as the paper towel and roll the two sheets up together, fastening the ends with paper clips. Place it on the wax paper with the other sheets. Place the supporting wax paper with the wet sheets in direct sunlight. A day later, observe the wetness of the sheets. The flat sheet should be dry; the folded sheet might have a damp spot or two near its bottom; the rolled-up sheet will have several damp spots; the wax-covered sheet will still be damp all over.

20. ANIMALS EXHALE CARBON DIOXIDE

Animals inhale oxygen and exhale carbon dioxide. Plants in turn absorb the carbon dioxide and generate oxygen, a mutually life-sustaining process. This is part of the reason that in fish tanks and marine habitats, plants are needed to oxygenate the water for fish, while fish produce the carbon dioxide needed for plants to manufacture food.

MATERIALS: goldfish, glass or jar, limewater

Limewater

- Place the goldfish in a glass of limewater and let students observe how in a short time the limewater turns milky white, indicating the presence of carbon dioxide. Place the fish promptly back into its own aquarium, so that it is not harmed.

21. CARBON DIOXIDE-OXYGEN CYCLE

Plants use carbon dioxide in their growth and produce oxygen as a by-product.

MATERIALS: jar with lid, soda water, elodea or other water plant, test tube, florist's clay, nail, hammer, small block of wood, matches, splint

- Set the water plants in a jar nearly full of water and set the jar in sunlight until bubbles appear on the plants. These are oxygen bubbles. During photosynthesis, a plant's food manufacturing process, plants use sunlight and chlorophyll to produce oxygen.

- Place a water plant in a jar containing soda water, which is rich in carbon dioxide. Allow the soda water to sit for at least half an hour before inserting the plant. Use the nail to pierce a hole in the jar lid. Place a small wooden block under the lid, and hit the nail with the hammer. Place the lid on the jar carefully; place an inverted test tube filled with soda water over the hole in the lid. Seal all contact edges with florist's clay. Place the jar in sunlight. After the plant begins to manufacture food, some water in the test tube will be replaced with oxygen. You can test for this oxygen by removing the test tube and inserting into it a glowing wooden splint. Light the splint, blow off the flame, and while it is still glowing insert it in the test tube. The splint will relight in the presence of oxygen.

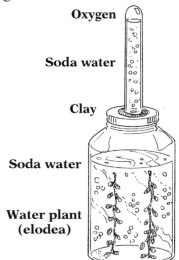

Oxygen

Soda water

Clay

Soda water

Water plant (elodea)

22. ANIMAL CIRCULATION

It is exciting for students to observe the **circulation** of live animals without harming them.

MATERIALS: small glass dish, cotton wrapping, water, goldfish, microscope

- Wrap a goldfish in a wet cotton wrapping, leaving the tail exposed, and place it in the dish. Focus the microscope on the tail of the fish (outside the wrappings) and observe the many capillaries. You will also notice red corpuscles moving in various directions. Those moving toward the tail are in arteries, while those moving in the opposite direction travel through veins. (Note that microscope images are reversed, so that something that appears to be traveling toward the tail is actually traveling away from it.) Be sure to return the goldfish to its own aquarium promptly, so that it is not harmed.

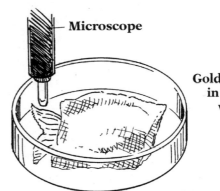

Microscope

Goldfish wrapped in wet cotton wrapping

23. PLANTS HAVE CIRCULATION (CAPILLARITY)

Water and other molecules tend to stick to their own kind. This is called **cohesion**. When molecules stick to other kinds of molecules, the process is called **adhesion**. When water or other substances enter very fine openings, they rise through a combination of cohesion and adhesion. This process is called **capillarity**. It explains how leaves of a very large tree can grow by drawing water from their roots, through the stems, and up through the trunk and the branches, until it finally reaches the foliage.

MATERIALS: small jar, water, red food coloring, celery stalk

- Half-fill the jar with a deep red solution of food coloring and water. Place a celery stalk in the jar. Let the setup stand for 15–20 minutes. Cut the celery stem above the water-line and observe the red color in its tubes.

Celery stalk

Red food coloring in water

Red color in tubes

24. CELL MODEL USING GELATIN

MATERIALS: small plastic box, water, package of gelatin, bean, plate

• Prepare the gelatin according to the instructions on the package. Pour the hot gelatin into the plastic box and let it cool. When the gelatin is nearly hardened, place the bean in the center of the gelatin. Let the gelatin harden. Flip the box over and lay the gelatin on a plate or other flat surface. Now you have a model of an animal cell with the nucleus (bean), the cytoplasm (gelatin) and the cell membrane (outer skin of gelatin).

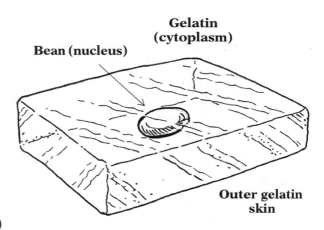

25. TESTING FOR STARCH IN FOODS

Carbohydrates are foods that contain the elements carbon, hydrogen, and oxygen. Examples of carbohydrates include starch, sugar, potatoes, vegetables, fruit, cereals, and legumes.

MATERIALS: Lugol's solution, bread, cracker, potato slice

• Lugol's solution is a brown liquid, containing iodine. Add a drop of Lugol's solution to a slice of bread, a cracker, or a slice of potato. If the Lugol's solution turns blue-black, then the substance contains starch.

26. TESTING FOR SUGAR IN FOODS

Benedict's solution is a bluish liquid. When it is heated in the presence of sugar, it changes in color from blue to green, yellow, orange, or red.

MATERIALS: Bunsen burner, Benedict's solution or Clinitest™, test tube, forceps, foods that contain sugar (fruit, cake, etc.)

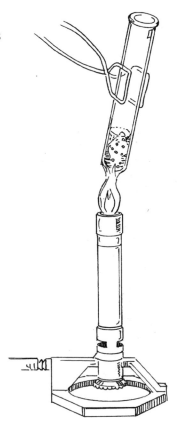

- Place the substance you wish to test in a test tube and add Benedict's solution. Using forceps, hold the test tube over the Bunsen burner. If the solution changes color as it is heated, the substance contains sugar.

- Alternatively, buy a package of Clinitest at a pharmacy or drug-store. (You may have to order it in advance.) Follow the directions on the package and test other foods for sugar. With Clinitest, you do not have to heat foods to test for sugar. As with most other indicators, you basically match colors.

27. TESTING FOR MINERALS IN FOODS

Most foods contain **minerals**. When burned, they leave a residue—a gray or whitish ash. The ash indicates the presence of minerals. If no ash is left, the food contained no minerals. The ashes show the presence of minerals but do not show which minerals. Other tests are available to test for specific minerals.

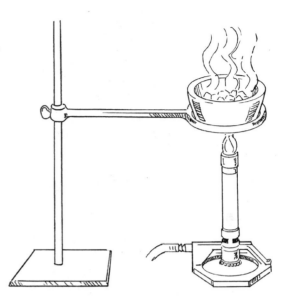

MATERIALS: small crucible, crucible support, ring with stand, Bunsen burner, food to be tested for minerals

- Place food to be tested in the crucible and heat until it either burns off or turns into ash.

28. TESTING FOR FATS IN FOODS

MATERIALS: brown paper bag, foods to be tested for fat

Overripe apple

Brown paper bag

- Rub the food to be tested on a brown paper bag. Most foods will cause a wet-looking spot. If the spot dries, the food contains no fat. If fats are present, the spot will not appear to dry up.

29. TESTING FOR PROTEIN IN FOODS #1

Proteins belong to a group of complex organic (carbon-containing) compounds that are an important part of the protoplasm (basic living cell). Proteins are an important component of the human diet. Knowing which foods are rich in protein can help you make the best selections for a healthy diet.

MATERIALS: copper sulfate, lime (garden lime), water, plate, two eyedroppers, two glass jars with covers, foods to be tested for protein—meat, peanut butter, cheese, slice of hard-boiled egg, carrot, piece of apple

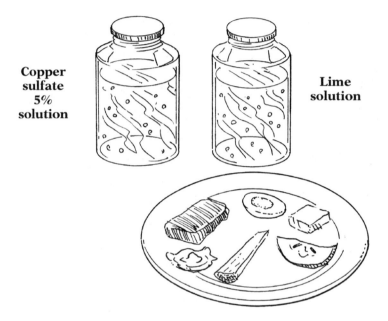

- Prepare in one jar a 5% solution of copper sulfate. In the other jar, prepare a lime solution: one cup of water to a tablespoon of lime. Place the foods to be tested on a plate. Add equal amounts of both solutions to each food to be tested. If a violet color appears, the food contains protein. A darker violet indicates more protein than a lighter violet.

30. TESTING FOR PROTEIN IN FOODS #2

Proteins are foods that contain the element nitrogen. Examples include meat, fish, fowl, eggs, and cheeses.

MATERIALS: Biuret solution, test tube, test tube rack, foods to be tested for protein

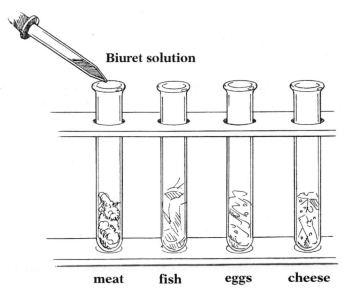

- Biuret solution is an indicator used to test for food proteins. Add food to the test tube, then add Biuret solution. If the solution changes from light blue to purple, then protein is present. The darker the purple, the more protein there is.

31. TESTING FOR VITAMIN C IN FOODS

Vitamin C is an essential vitamin that helps living cells to grow and reproduce. The human body needs a good supply of vitamin C if it is to function properly. A vitamin C deficiency results in **scurvy**, a serious ailment. It starts with bleeding gums and tooth loss, and was the dreaded scourge of sailors in centuries past. Since vitamin C is water soluble and does not accumulate in the human body, we need a fresh supply of it on a daily basis. Citrus fruits and bell peppers are good sources of vitamin C.

MATERIALS: indophenol, test tube, food to be tested

- Indophenol is an indicator used to test for vitamin C. Place about one inch of indophenol in a test tube. Add a small amount of food, a drop at a time, to the indophenol. Shake well after each drop. Indophenol is light blue and will turn colorless in the presence of vitamin C.

32. TESTING FOR WATER IN FOODS

MATERIALS: test tube, forceps, food sample, Bunsen burner

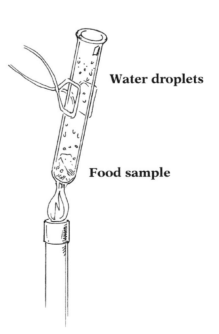

Water droplets

Food sample

- Place a small sample of food in a dry test tube and heat the test tube gently. If droplets of water form on the inside of the test tube, there is water in the food. If no water droplets form inside the test tube, the food does not contain water.

33. TESTING FOR SALT

MATERIALS: test tube, silver nitrate, salt, water

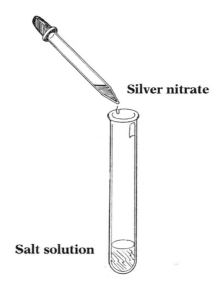

Silver nitrate

Salt solution

- Prepare a few milliliters of salt solution in the test tube. Add a few drops of silver nitrate and observe the solid that is formed. The solid indicates the presence of salt.

34. CHLOROPHYLL AND CHROMATOGRAPHY

Plant chloroplasts contain **chlorophyll**. This gives plants their characteristic green color. Food-making in a plant takes place when the sun's energy reaches the chloroplasts to produce sugar from carbon dioxide and water. This process is called **photosynthesis**. Without chlorophyll, the process cannot take place. To study chlorophyll, scientists separate the chlorophyll from its source leaves. This process, called **chromatography**, can be simulated in this activity.

MATERIALS: beaker, alcohol, paper towel, ink or food color

Ink dot

Alcohol

- Cut a strip of paper towel about one inch wide and six inches long. About three inches from the bottom, place a dot of ink or food color. Tape the strip to the inside edge of the glass and pour about half an inch of alcohol into the glass. Look at the strip five minutes later. Notice how this process separates the elements of the ink. Chlorophyll is studied in a similar manner, but obtaining a chromatogram that will separate chlorophyll requires a lengthy chlorophyll separation process.

35. BIODEGRADABLE MATERIALS

In the earth's environment, materials decompose through natural means, **biodegradation**. Many manufactured chemicals used in farming, food preservation, and other everyday applications prevent this natural breakdown. A red maraschino cherry will not decompose, as it has been treated with preservatives that inhibit biodegradation.

MATERIALS: two plastic milk carton bottoms (gallon size), dirt, maraschino cherry, piece of bread or fruit, water

Milk cartons with dirt

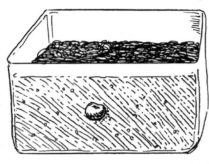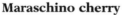

Maraschino cherry   **Bread slice**

- Half-fill the bottoms of both milk cartons with dirt. Place a maraschino cherry in one, a piece of bread or fruit in the other. Cover both with dirt. Keep the soil moist by watering regularly. Keep a log of watering dates and depth of samples. At the end of one month, look for what you buried. The cherry will have changed color but will be intact, while the bread or fruit will have decomposed. Write comments on the status of the samples when unearthed.

36. VITAMINS: THEIR IMPORTANCE TO US

Vitamins, nutrients found mainly in plants or in plant-eating animals, affect human health. Here is a brief summary of key diseases caused by vitamin deficiency in the diet:

VITAMIN	DEFICIENCY DISEASES
A	Hard, dry skin, night blindness
B_1	Beriberi
B complex	Neurological disorders
C	Scurvy
D	Rickets
E	Severe circulatory problems
K	Poor or no blood clotting

- Read to class the labels of a bottle of a multivitamin supplement.

- Read students the labels on several food packages.

- Have students research the various vitamin-deficiency diseases and have them make brief reports.

37. MINERALS: THEIR IMPORTANCE TO US

Minerals are chemicals that are essential for life. A shortage of minerals in the human diet causes severe problems. A deficiency of iron causes **anemia**. A deficiency of iodine causes the thyroid gland to swell, called **goiter**. Iodine is added to salt in the United States.

Here is a summary of a few minerals and their uses:

MINERALS	KEY USES
Sodium	Keeps muscles and nerves healthy
Potassium	Keeps muscles and nerves healthy
Calcium	Building block for teeth and bones
Phosphorus	Keeps teeth, bones, and brain healthy
Iodine	Controls human metabolism (oxidation)
Trace metals (Zinc, etc.)	Maintains healthy body functions
Iron	Helps build red blood cells and prevents anemia

- Read to students the labels of several vitamin-plus-mineral bottles.

- Read to students the labels on several food packages.

- Have students research minerals and their deficiency-related problems and have them make brief reports.

38. SEPARATING OUT IRON FROM CREAM OF WHEAT

Iron is a key mineral added to the human diet to assist the body with the manufacture of red blood cells. According to research, women need more iron than men.

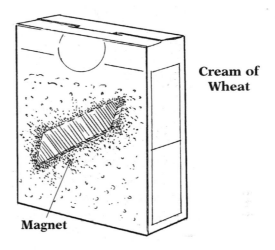

Cream of Wheat

Magnet

MATERIALS: box of Cream of Wheat™, magnet

- Place the magnet inside the box of Cream of Wheat, close the box, and shake it for a couple of minutes. Have your students observe the iron that collects on the magnet.

39. PERISTALSIS

The digestive track is made of many tissues, and among these is muscle tissue. **Peristalsis** is the muscular action in the digestive track that moves the food along its way.

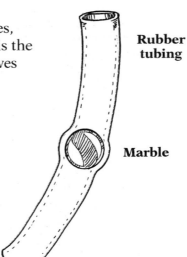

Rubber tubing

Marble

MATERIALS: rubber tubing, marble

- Find a length of rubber tubing that is not wider than a marble. Place the marble inside the tube and move it along by squeezing the tube.

40. MECHANICAL DIGESTION

MATERIALS: small chopping block, celery or apple, sharp knife, two test tubes, sugar cubes, granulated sugar, water

- Chop apple or celery into fine pieces to simulate the action of teeth in the mouth.

- Fill both test tubes about three-quarters full of water. Add a sugar cube to one and some granulated sugar to the other. Shake both for a few seconds and observe how much longer it takes to dissolve the sugar cube. Breaking food down mechanically allows it to be absorbed more quickly into the digestive system.

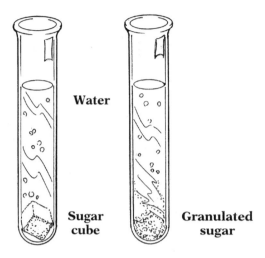

Water

Sugar cube

Granulated sugar

41. CHEMICAL DIGESTION

Chemical digestion breaks food molecules into smaller ones, to allow the nutrients to be absorbed by the body. Saliva in the mouth lubricates and wets the food to allow it to move through the digestive tract; it also provides **enzymes**, chemicals made by the body to help break down the food. Saliva enzymes digest starch and change it into sugar.

MATERIALS: piece of bread or cracker for each student

- Give each student either a piece of bread or a cracker to chew. Have them chew for about two or three minutes without swallowing. The bread or cracker will taste sweeter. This is a good example of chemical digestion. (See the following demonstration for a lab test of this process.)

Bread or cracker

42. PREDIGESTING FOOD IN THE MOUTH

Demonstration 41, Chemical Digestion, showed informally that enzymes in saliva convert starch into sugar. This lab gives a formal demonstration of the same thing.

MATERIALS: four test tubes, starch, water, Benedict's solution, Lugol's solution (iodine), Bunsen burner, forceps, saliva

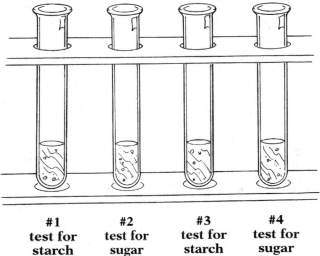

#1	#2	#3	#4
test for starch	test for sugar	test for starch	test for sugar

- Place a small amount of starch in each of the four test tubes. Assign each tube a number from 1 to 4. Fill each one-quarter full of water, and shake to mix the contents.

1. Use iodine to test tube #1 for starch. It will confirm that starch is indeed present.

2. Use Benedict's solution to test tube #2 for sugar. (For details, see Demonstration 26, Testing for Sugar in Foods, page 22.) The test will confirm that test tube #2 does not contain sugar. Test tubes #1 and #2 form your control group.

3. Now place some saliva in the remaining two test tubes. Shake them well. Use iodine to test #3 for starch. The result will be negative—starch is not present.

4. Test #4 for sugar. The result will show that it contains sugar. The enzymes in the saliva have changed some of the starch into sugar.

43. DIGESTION

While the saliva in the mouth contains one enzyme that changes starch into sugar, other nutrients must be separated too. The stomach produces gastric juices that lubricate the food so that it can move along. Gastric juices contain the two enzymes: **rennin** and **pepsin**. In addition, they contain **hydrochloric acid** (HCl) and water. The acid kills bacteria and dissolves minerals.

MATERIALS: chicken bone, piece of string, beaker, **diluted** hydrochloric acid, safety gloves, soap and water

> **CAUTION!** Hydrochloric acid is corrosive.

- Suspend the chicken bone in the diluted hydrochloric acid for several days. Pull it out, then wash it well to remove any residual acid. Now show your students how the bone has become soft and rubbery. The acid has dissolved some of the minerals in the bone.

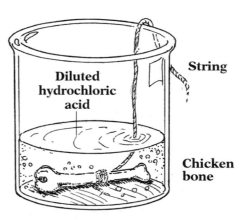

String

Diluted hydrochloric acid

Chicken bone

44. STOMACH CHEMISTRY: PEPSIN AND HYDROCHLORIC ACID

Gastric juices contain water, hydrochloric acid, pepsin, and rennin. Rennin is an enzyme that breaks down **casein**, or milk protein. The enzyme pepsin, together with hydrochloric acid, breaks down large protein molecules into smaller ones.

MATERIALS: four test tubes, test tube holder, **diluted** hydrochloric acid, hard-boiled egg, water, pepsin, safety gloves

- Proceed with the following steps.

1. Place four test tubes in a holder and label them #1, #2, #3, and #4.

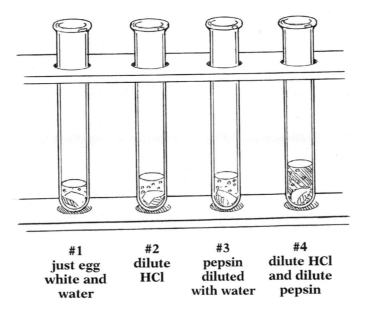

#1	#2	#3	#4
just egg white and water	dilute HCl	pepsin diluted with water	dilute HCl and dilute pepsin

2. Place a small piece of egg white (a protein) in each tube and cover it with water. Test tube #1 will act as your control.

3. Place some diluted hydrochloric acid in test tube #2.

4. Place some pepsin diluted with water in test tube #3.

5. Place both diluted hydrochloric acid and diluted pepsin in test tube #4.

6. Examine the four test tubes one day later. You will observe that the egg white in #1 and #2 has not changed. Some egg is left in #3, while most of the egg in #4 has been digested. This verifies that pepsin and hydrochloric acids are synergetic: They work better together than either one works alone.

45. HEAT AIDS DIGESTION

Heat is a key element in food digestion.

MATERIALS: three test tubes, diluted pepsin, **diluted** hydrochloric acid, incubator, refrigerator, hard-boiled egg, safety gloves

All three—Egg + diluted pepsin + diluted hydrochloric acid

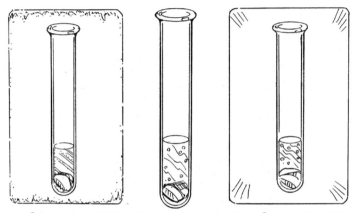

Refrigerator 40°F   Room temp.   Incubator 98.6°F

- Place nearly equal amounts of egg white in the three test tubes. Add to each tube equal amounts of pepsin and hydrochloric acid. Store one tube overnight in the refrigerator, one at room temperature, and one in the incubator at 37°C or 98.6°F, human body temperature. You will be able to show students that the warmest tube shows the most digestion.

46. BILE: AN EMULSIFIER FOR FATS

Fats and oils are digested in the small intestine with the help of **lipase**, an enzyme. **Bile**, produced by the liver, is a greenish liquid stored in the gall bladder. Bile is not an enzyme but an **emulsifier**. Bile helps break down large fat drops into tiny fat droplets, dispersing them evenly through the small intestine (**emulsification**). Emulsification can be produced mechanically by beating the fat molecules and breaking them into small particles. This process is known as **homogenization**. Milk is usually sold homogenized. Without homogenizing, all the butterfat would float to the top of the bottle.

MATERIALS: two test tubes, bile, water, salad oil, dropper, liquid detergent (If bile is not available, use a couple of drops of liquid detergent in water.)

- Half-fill one test tube with bile. Half-fill the other tube with water. Add a couple of drops of oil to both, and shake. Notice how the oil floats in the water after you stop shaking, while the bile forms a cloudy mixture with the oil. Bile works in the same way during digestion in the small intestine.

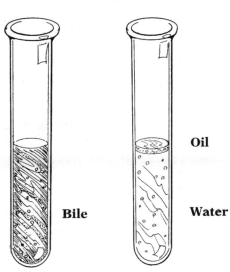

47. MODEL OF THE SMALL INTESTINE

The small intestine is not smooth but covered by millions of tiny fingerlike structures called **villi**. Villi contain **capillaries** and **lacteals**. The proteins and sugars pass into the capillaries, while fats pass through the lacteals. All food materials that pass through the capillaries and lacteals enter the bloodstream, where they can be used by the body as energy. Fats are stored as reserve energy; proteins go to repair and build new cells; carbohydrates provide heat and muscle energy.

MATERIALS: glass jar, coffee filter, water, salt or sugar

- Fill the glass jar with water. Place about a tablespoon of sugar or salt in the coffee filter. Fold the filter into a small bag and wet its upper end. Place the filter bag into the jar and fold the wet end of the bag over the lip of the jar.

You will observe a wavelike action coming out of the bag, almost like rain. This process is called **osmosis**. Substances move from a region of higher osmotic pressure to a region of lower pressure through a porous membrane. The sugar solution has more osmotic pressure than plain water, so it moves through the filter into the plain water. This demonstrates the action of villi.

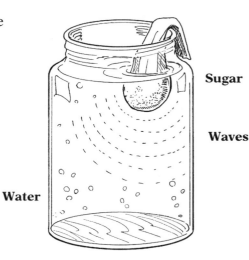

48. THE HEARTBEAT AND PULSE

Every time the heart beats, blood spurts into the arteries. If you feel an artery near a bone or near the surface of the skin, you can feel these spurts as pulses. The pulses and the heartbeat are the same. The normal heartbeat for a person at rest is 70 beats per minute. A mouse has a heartbeat of 1000, while an elephant has one of 25. Generally, the smaller the animal, the greater the number of heartbeats per minute.

MATERIALS: stethoscope, watch with second hand, microphone, amplifier, speakers

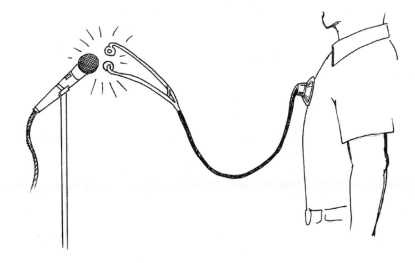

- Place the stethoscope on a student's heart and have students listen to it. If you have a microphone with an amplifier and speakers, place the earpiece of the stethoscope near the microphone and everyone will be able to hear the heart beating.

- Have students take their own pulse.

49. NICOTINE SPEEDS UP HEARTBEAT

Nicotine, a strong and highly addictive stimulant found in cigarettes, increases a person's heartbeat rate.

**1 jump
per second**   **2 jumps
per second**

- Have students stand by their desks and move their chairs out of the way. Have them jump up once every second for about half a minute. Repeat the activity but double the speed of jumps, so that students jump up twice in each second. Students will quickly become nearly exhausted. Parallel the increase in jumping speed with the increase of heartbeats when nicotine is present. An increase of 30 heartbeats per minutes means 43,200 extra heartbeats per day and 15,768,000 per year. These extra heartbeats place unneeded, damaging stress on the human heart muscle.

50. NICOTINE AND LIVING THINGS

MATERIALS: beaker, water, graduated cylinder, strainer or filter, marking pencil, eyedropper, nicotine solution, clock with second hand, guppy, overhead projector

- In preparation:

1. Make the nicotine solution by soaking the tobacco of a cigarette in 15–20 milliliters of water for a couple of hours.

2. Strain or filter the tobacco solution.

- Mark the front of the beaker with a vertical line. Fill the beaker with water and add the guppy. Let it swim around for a couple of minutes. Count and record how many times the fish swims around in one minute. Obtain the average of several tries. Place 18–20 drops of nicotine solution in the beaker water. Count how many times the fish swims around in one minute. Obtain the average of several tries. Promptly return the fish to plain water, so it will not be harmed. For clearer viewing, place the beaker on top of an overhead projector for bottom illumination.

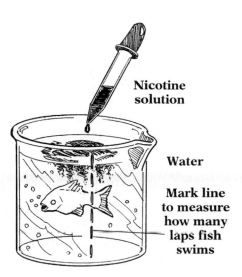

Nicotine solution

Water

Mark line to measure how many laps fish swims

51. INDOOR PLANT INFESTATION: NICOTINE SPRAY FOR PLANTS

Indoor plants sometimes do poorly because of infestation by insects such as aphids. You will prepare a colloidal soap solution that will affect the spiracles of aphids. A **colloid solution** consists of very fine particles of a substance suspended in another substance. Soap spreads the solution, for it is a good wetting agent. It breaks down the surface tension of the liquid and clogs the aphids' and other sucking insects' spiracles.

MATERIALS: plant infested with aphids, cigarette, water, tablespoon, small beaker, hot plate, measuring cup, soap solution, eyedropper, small sprayer

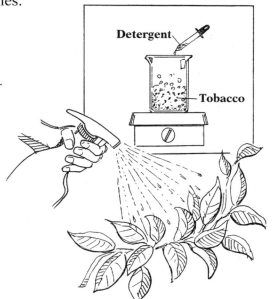

- Place 2–3 tablespoons of water in the beaker. Add the tobacco from a cigarette and boil for 8–10 minutes. Add enough water to make a cupful of solution. Add a few drops of liquid detergent. Mix and spray on the infested plant. Within a few days, students should observe a marked reduction in the level of infestation.

52. BIOLOGICAL CONTROL OF PESTS

When a crop is infested by pests, two choices are available to the grower: using pesticides, or introducing a predator species to provide biological control. In this activity, a rose cutting infested with aphids will have biological control through the use of a ladybug, a carnivore. One of the ladybug's favorite foods is the aphid greenfly.

MATERIALS: small bottle, soap, water, glass jar, rubber band, cheesecloth, aphid-infested rosebush cutting, small clippers, ladybug(s)

- Wash both the bottle and the jar with soap and rinse well. Cut a rose with several aphid-infested leaves, about four inches in length. Place some water in the bottle, then insert the rose so that the leaves are outside the bottle. Place the bottle with the rose cutting inside the larger jar. Gently place a ladybug inside the jar. Cover the jar with cheesecloth and secure it with a rubber band. Observe for several days. You will notice a major drop in the aphid population. Release the ladybug outdoors at the end of the demonstration.

Ladybug
Aphids

53. ASTHMA AND EMPHYSEMA

Many people suffer from the lung disorder **asthma**. The word comes from Greek and means "panting." Asthma is usually caused by some irritant to the small air tubes in the lungs. To ease the symptoms of asthma, drugs can be used to relax the muscles of the air tubes. **Emphysema**, another lung disorder, occurs when the alveoli in the lungs break or become nonfunctional. It is often a side effect of smoking. For emphysema, an irreversible condition, oxygen is the only resource. Breaths become gradually shallower (smaller) and use nearly all the energy of the afflicted individual.

MATERIALS: drinking straw for each student

- Provide all students with a drinking straw and ask them to pinch their noses closed. Ask them to try to breathe only through the straw for three minutes. Warn them that if they feel faint or dizzy, they should stop at once. Monitor students carefully to watch for any signs of faintness.

54. KEEPING COOL

The human body is a chemical factory, with oxidation taking place all the time. The body temperature is carefully regulated. The body sweats a combination of water and salt. This allows water to evaporate, which cools the skin and maintains the body at 98.6°F, or 37°C. A liquid that changes to a gas absorbs heat energy (heat of vaporization). When air is saturated with water vapor, humidity, perspiration cannot evaporate and individuals suffer from heat. Meteorologists use a comfort index, made up of the combination of temperature and moisture in the air, to arrive at a true relative temperature. This is the temperature as it is perceived by humans. Alcohol also needs heat to evaporate. While skin provides the heat, the sensation of alcohol on the skin is one of relative cooling.

MATERIALS: dropper, rubbing alcohol

- Have students line up. Place one drop of alcohol on the back of each student's hand. Have students take note of the cool feeling where you placed the alcohol drop.

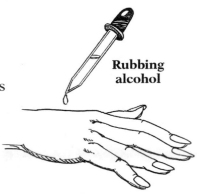

Rubbing alcohol

55. REDI'S EXPERIMENT: SOURCE OF LIVING THINGS

In the 1600's, Italian physician Francesco Redi observed the presence of worms on rotten meat. In time, he discovered that these were not really worms but the **larvae** of flies that had hatched from eggs deposited by other flies. By placing a screen over the meat and preventing flies from reaching it, Redi showed that the meat did not contain worms or flies. He was able to demonstrate that flies come from flies, goats from goats, etc.

MATERIALS: three glass jars, three rubber bands, plastic covering, gauze, meat

- Place a small amount of meat in each jar. Cover one jar with gauze, one with plastic wrap, and leave the last one uncovered. Place all three jars in a sunny window. After several days,

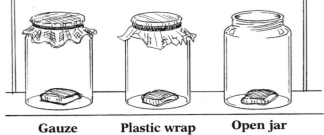

Gauze　　　**Plastic wrap**　　　**Open jar**

examine the results. They should replicate Redi's findings.

56. ASEXUAL REPRODUCTION: BUDDING (YEAST CELLS AND BREAD)

Asexual reproduction means that only one organism is needed to produce an offspring. Yeast reproduces itself asexually by **budding**; that is, two cells of different size are produced. Yeast is a microscopic one-cell plant. In budding, the cell wall pushes out, beginning the bud. The cell nucleus moves toward the bud and divides, with one nucleus moving into the bud and the other remaining in the parent cell. The bud grows, and eventually a cell wall grows between the parent cell and the bud. Finally the bud breaks away and develops into a mature cell. If you combine sugar with flour, water, and yeast, the yeast cells will oxidize the sugar, producing alcohol and carbon dioxide in a process called **fermentation**. During baking, the alcohol evaporates. Carbon dioxide forms bubbles in the dough, causing the bread to rise. This process makes bread soft and spongy.

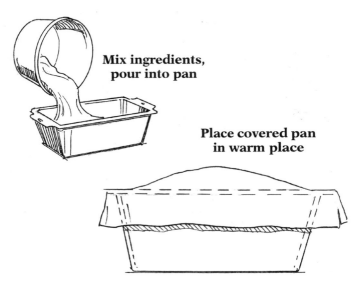

Mix ingredients, pour into pan

Place covered pan in warm place

MATERIALS: flour, sugar, water, yeast, bread recipe, bowl, pan

- Following any standard bread recipe, mix all the ingredients in a bowl and then pour the dough into a pan. Cover the pan with a cloth, and set it in a warm place for most of the class period. Have students observe how the dough increases in size due to the action of the yeast.

57. ASEXUAL REPRODUCTION: SPORULATION (SPORES AND MOLDS)

Bread mold under a microscope appears as many long stalks, each with a ball ending. Each ball is a spore case and contains thousands of cells called **spores**. Spores are the reproductive cells of molds. Each cell can grow into a new mold. The bread provides the nutrients for the growth of molds. When the ball that holds the spores (the spore case) breaks, **sporulation** (another form of asexual reproduction) takes place and the spores grow into new plants.

MATERIALS: bread, jar, two slides, microscope

- Place a piece of bread in the jar and let it stay uncovered until mold forms on the bread. This will take place in a couple of days. Prepare a slide and show students the mold and the spore cases.

58. ASEXUAL REPRODUCTION: VEGETATIVE PROPAGATION

Sometimes, growing parts of plants develop into new plants. This form of asexual reproduction is called **vegetative propagation**. A potato is an underground stem known as a tuber. A potato grows many small eyes, which when planted develop into new potato plants.

MATERIALS: several potatoes, pot, soil, water

- Let the potatoes develop eyes, then plant them in the pot. Water lightly. Observe the growth of several new potato plants.

59. SEXUAL REPRODUCTION

Preceding activities demonstrate asexual reproduction, in which only one parent is necessary. Seeds are the product of sexual reproduction. Germination is the process of growth for the embryo inside the seed.

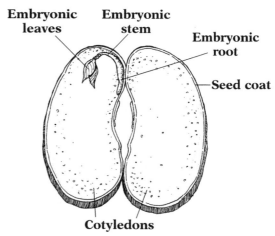

- Take a seed like a bean and soak it overnight. Its coat becomes soft and can be peeled off quite easily. The two halves contain food, which is generally starch (a quick iodine test will prove this). Attached to one half of the bean is the embryo. Seeds are formed by the fertilization of an ovule by a pollen cell. After fertilization, the ovule becomes a seed. A new plant can grow from the seed.

- You can also use Demonstration 3, Phototropism #1: Plants Grow Toward Light, on page 3. Have your students make daily observations to see how the seeds sprout.

60. INSECT MULTIPLICATION: FRUIT FLIES

Fruit flies are a good example of rapid insect multiplication. If left unchecked, insects would overrun the world.

MATERIALS: two pint or quart jars with covers, grapes or ripe banana, cotton covering

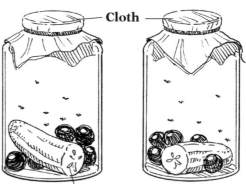

- Place a piece of ripe banana and/or several grapes in both jars, cover, and place in a warm room, **not** in sunlight. Keep track of the flies in each bottle daily for eight to ten days. Students should observe and record the increase of fruit flies, then calculate and project the increase over months and years. The numbers will be astounding.

61. INSECT MULTIPLICATION: GENERATIONS

The life cycle of a fruit fly is so short that a few weeks can produce multiple generations. Larvae emerge from eggs in one or two days, then pupate for about five days to change into adults and mate. Female fruit flies are larger than males and have a bigger abdomen. Males have a black-tipped abdomen.

MATERIALS: one or two glass jars, ripe banana or other fruit, crumpled paper, magnifying glass, test tubes, foil

- Place the ripe fruit in the jar and let it sit in the open until fruit flies appear; they may have either entered the jar or hatched from eggs on the fruit. Place a piece of crumpled paper inside the jar, then cover the jar with absorbent cotton. You will observe larvae, pupae, and adult fruit flies in less than two weeks. The jar will contain the fruit flies that were caught and the new generation of flies. You can continue by preparing another habitat jar and by raising grandchildren. To observe fruit flies closely, place them in test tubes. Wrap the test tubes in foil and open small areas for observation. The fruit flies will come to the openings, attracted by the light. Use the magnifying glass to observe details.

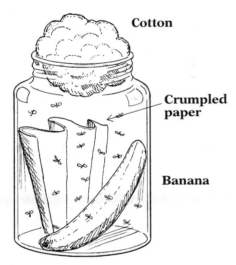

Cotton

Crumpled paper

Banana

62. INHERITED TRAITS

The general appearance of people or animals provides clues to many inherited characteristics called **traits**. While families share many traits, specific characteristics are uniquely individual. Examples of traits include height (short, medium, tall), hair color (brown, black, blond, red), eye color (brown, blue, hazel), and frame size (small, medium large).

MATERIALS: family pictures (Ask each student to bring in one.)

- Have students write out as many traits as possible that are common in their family.

63. ENVIRONMENT AFFECTS EXPRESSION OF GENES

Traits are inherited through **genes**. Genes represent a person's total inherited potential, if the environment allows for the genes' full expression. When the environment is restricted, the genes do not change but the development of traits is stunted.

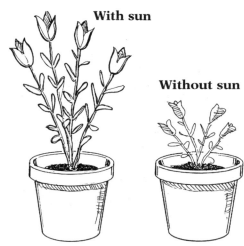

With sun

Without sun

MATERIALS: two small potted plants, water, fertilizer

- Take two small plants and let one develop to its full potential with abundant sunshine, water, and fertilizer. Treat the second plant the same, but keep it in the shade. You will notice a major discrepancy in traits. The difference is due to the environment.

64. FISH AND COLOR

Fish, like other living things, have preferences for color, moisture, temperature, and other variables. Their preferences are transferred into their habitat (environment). Coniferous plants like certain altitudes. Marine life is extremely temperature sensitive. If the water temperature changes by as little as 1°F, many fish will leave an area.

MATERIALS: fish tank, water, several varieties of fish, colored cards or papers, tape

Colored paper

- Select one variety of fish and place some in the tank, after creating a suitable habitat. Tape a colored card or paper to the outside of the glass tank and have students count the number of fish that congregate near it over a set time. Have them check to see if the fish have color preferences. This will answer the age-old question of whether fish see colors.

- Repeat this demonstration with different varieties of fish.

65. VARIABLES AFFECT HABITAT

All living plants and animals have preferences for color, moisture, temperature, and other life-affecting variables. Their preferences are transferred into their habitat.

MATERIALS: worms, paper of different colors, water

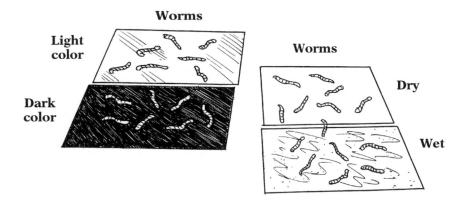

- Place the worms on two cards of different colors, one light and one dark. Notice which card most worms migrate toward.

- Again place the worms on two cards, one moist, one dry. Observe the mass migration to one of the cards.

- This demonstration can be repeated to test for many other variables such as acid, base, odor, temperature, etc.

66. EARTHWORMS

Earthworms, known as night crawlers, move through earth. They do this by making the front of their segmented body longer and contracting the back part. Since earthworms live underground, we rarely see them moving. In this activity, you will build a wormery and observe how earthworms crawl around.

MATERIALS: damp soil, large empty glass jar (no lid needed), clean sand, leaves, garden spade, three or four earthworms, rubber band, cheesecloth, black construction paper, sealing tape

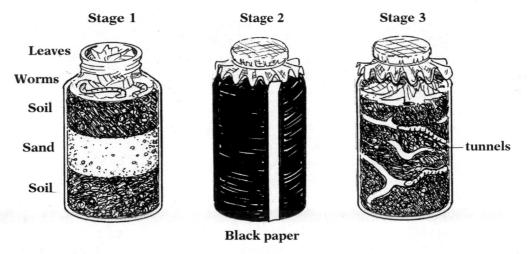

- Place a layer of damp soil on the bottom of the jar. Add to this a layer of clean sand, then add more damp soil. Using the spade, dig in moist, warm spots in a garden to unearth several earthworms. Collect a few green leaves. Place the worms and the leaves in the jar on top of the soil. Cover the jar with cheesecloth, secured with the rubber band. Wrap the entire jar in black construction paper, making certain to overlap the edges. Seal it with tape. Set the jar in a safe place. After a few days, remove the black paper and observe the worm burrows. You will see tunnels through the soil and the sand.

67. THE LIFE OF EARTHWORMS

Earthworms like a moist, dark environment. They will tunnel into the soil only after everything is dark. In the process of tunneling, they pass the soil through their bodies, remove the nutrients, and deposit a substance called **castings**. Earthworm tunnels aerate the soil, and the castings enrich it.

MATERIALS: tall, thin tin can (open at one end), large clear glass or plastic jar, earthworms, rich soil, sand, water, piece of black paper, tape

- Have your students look at an earthworm and try to decide which end is the head and which end is the tail. Place the can inside the jar, closed end up. (The can is introduced so that earthworms are forced to tunnel near the surfaces of the clear jar.) Fill the jar with the soil, up to the top of the can. Add a thin layer of sand on top of the soil. Moisten the soil but do not overwater. Place the earthworms in the jar. Wrap the entire jar in black paper, making sure the ends overlap, then seal. Leave the jar for several days. When you remove the black paper, you will observe worm castings on top of the layer of sand in the jar.

68. METAMORPHOSIS

Many species of insects go through a complete **metamorphosis**, where their larvae bear a resemblance to true worms. This is true of mealworms. A mealworm is the larva of one of many grain-eating beetles. Metamorphosis is clearly demonstrated by mealworms changing into beetles.

MATERIALS: glass jar, clear plastic, grain cereal, mealworms

- Put grain cereal in a jar and place the mealworms on it. Cover the jar with plastic and stand it in plain view. Do not forget to poke several airholes in the plastic. Depending on the room temperature, the mealworms will change into beetles in one or two weeks. This is a good example of metamorphosis with a commonly available animal.

Plastic wrap

Mealworms

Grain cereal

69. SOUNDS PEOPLE HEAR

People listen to sounds all the time. If they concentrate, they can discriminate between sounds and can recognize secondary ones mixed with the dominant ones.

MATERIALS: tape recorder, audiotape, common sounds

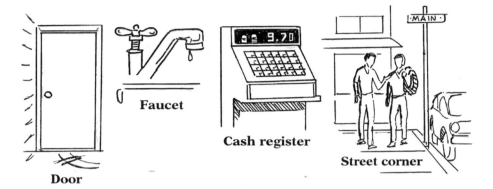

Faucet

Cash register

Street corner

Door

- Prepare an audiotape with many different sounds like a door closing, a refrigerator door closing, a door slamming, a water faucet opening and closing, a busy street corner, a market checkout lane, and other common sounds. Have students listen to the tape for about five minutes and have them write down as many different sounds as they can recognize. Have them share their experience with others. Replay the tape to confirm their answers.

70. HOW MUCH SOIL PLANTS USE

During their lifetime, plants use up only traces of minerals from the soil. Their extensive growth is made possible by their production of food from inorganic materials, water in the soil, and carbon dioxide.

MATERIALS: small flowerpot, potting soil, seeds, water, scale

- Weigh the amount of soil needed to fill the pot. Weigh the seeds. Plant the seeds in the potting soil and water it. Wait until the plants are several inches tall. Remove them, making sure that you brush off into the pot all the soil from their roots. Now reweigh the soil and the plants. Compare their weights with the original figures.

71. HYDROPONICS

Hydroponics is the science of growing plants primarily in a nutrient solution in water, without soil. This method of plant growth was discovered in the 1800's when scientists were trying to study the nutritional needs and root systems of plants. There are two types of hydroponics: **water culture** and **aggregate culture**. In a water culture, the plants are suspended over a bed of nutrient solution. As the plants grow, the roots reach into the nutrient solution. In an aggregate culture, the plants are held in coarse materials such as sand and gravel and the nutrient solution is constantly circulated in the anchoring materials. You might want to try out different combinations of nutrients as your project grows. Tomatoes do particularly well in hydroponics. Follow the instructions carefully.

MATERIALS: aquarium, wire mesh, wire mesh cutter, water, $2\frac{3}{4}$ gallons distilled water, small sack sphagnum moss (peat moss), 2 tsp calcium nitrate, $\frac{1}{4}$ tsp ammonium nitrate, $\frac{1}{4}$ tsp ammonium sulfate, $1\frac{1}{4}$ tsp Epsom salts, $\frac{1}{2}$ tsp potassium acid phosphate, $\frac{1}{8}$ tsp boric acid, $\frac{1}{8}$ tsp manganese sulfate, $\frac{1}{8}$ tsp zinc sulfate, $\frac{1}{8}$ tsp ferrous sulfate, bean and corn seeds, measuring cup, set measuring spoons, stirrer

1. Cut the wire mesh so that it is as wide as the aquarium, and eight inches longer. Four inches from each end, bend the wire mesh at right angles to form a platform the same length as the aquarium, with four-inch uprights. Place the mesh platform inside the tank. The uprights should keep it about four inches above the base of the tank. (See diagram.)

2. Prepare three solutions; #1, #2, and #3. Only #1 will go into the aquarium, at the very end.

* Make solution #1 by dissolving in a cup of water:

   $\frac{1}{4}$ teaspoon ammonium sulfate

   $\frac{1}{2}$ teaspoon potassium acid phosphate

   $1\frac{1}{4}$ teaspoons Epsom salts

   2 teaspoons calcium nitrate

   When all the above are dissolved, add the solution to $2\frac{1}{2}$ gallons of distilled water and label it Solution #1.

* Make solution #2 by dissolving in a cup of water:

   $\frac{1}{8}$ teaspoon zinc sulfate

$\frac{1}{8}$ teaspoon manganese sulfate

$\frac{1}{8}$ teaspoon boric acid

When all are dissolved, label it Solution #2.

- Make solution #3 by dissolving in a cup of water:

  $\frac{1}{8}$ teaspoon ferrous sulfate

  When it is dissolved, label it Solution #3.

- Add 1 teaspoon of Solution #2 to Solution #1.

- Add 3 tablespoons of Solution #3 to Solution #1.

3. Pour the final Solution #1 (mixture) into the aquarium up to the level of the wire mesh platform.

4. Sprinkle a layer of peat moss (sphagnum moss) over the wire mesh platform.

5. Place bean and corn seeds on top of the peat moss.

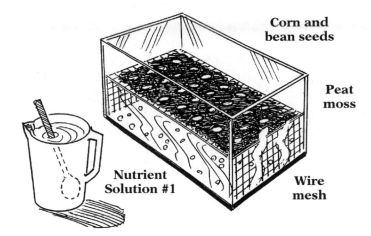

Over the next few days, the seeds will germinate and their roots will reach into the nutrient solution. Maintain the level of the nutrient by adding Solution #1 to keep it to the level of the wire platform. If needed, make more solution.

72. MOLDS

A **mold** is a simple organism belonging to the fungus family. Since molds cannot make their own food, they exist as parasites on plants and animals. Molds are useful in many ways. Many cheeses depend on molds for their ripening. Blue cheese is one example. Molds are present in many fertilizers. Antibiotics such as penicillin are derived from molds. In this demonstration you will grow a variety of molds.

MATERIALS: three clean glass jars with covers, plate, slice of bread, bruised pear, bruised apple, water

Bread   **Apple**   **Pear**

- Place the slice of bread on a plate and leave in the air for about an hour. Mold spores will fall on it from the air. Then place the slice of bread in a jar, sprinkle it lightly with water, and close the jar. Place the bruised apple in a jar and close it. Do the same with the pear. Place the three jars in a warm, dark place. After one week, bring them out and examine them. The molds working on the fruits will have rotted them. The bread will be covered with a cottonlike growth with white stalks and black balls at the ends. These are spore cases. Following the examination, discard the unopened jars.

73. REDUCING SOIL EROSION WITH PLANTS

Erosion is the process of breaking down and carrying away the materials of earth, such as rocks and soil. Erosion takes place slowly. Thousands of years of glacial erosion have created many North American mountain ranges. The Grand Canyon is a spectacular result of erosion. The Colorado River carved out its contours over millions of years. Erosion starts with the process of weathering. Here, earth materials are broken down into smaller pieces. The movement of water and air and the heat of the sun all contribute to weathering. Once the materials are loosened, water and wind can carry them to new locations. Heavy winds can blow soil and rocky substances over great distances, and heavy rains can wash soil particles downhill. Intensive farming can be an additional cause of soil erosion. When the soil is cleared of plants and trees, all its shields from wind and rain are removed. Now topsoil is at risk of being washed or blown away. To limit the erosion of topsoil, farmers plant cover crops such as alfalfa or grass or use tillage of the soil. Tilling allows old crops to remain on the surface of the soil.

In this demonstration you will observe some common approaches to reducing soil erosion.

MATERIALS: scrap pieces of wood 2 × 4, plastic or rubber tubing, florist's clay, scissors, topsoil, clay, sand, three glass or plastic bowls, three aluminum foil cake pans, cereal grain seeds, sprinkling can, water

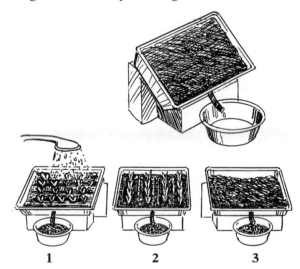

• Use the scissors to cut a small hole near the top of each of the three aluminum foil cake pans, in the middle of the longer side. Insert in each hole a 10-inch piece of tubing, and seal it with florist's clay. The holes can be larger than the tubing. Fill each pan with a layer of clay, a layer of topsoil, a layer of sand, and a final layer of topsoil. With the hose pointing down, place the three pans at an angle of about 30° by placing them over a block, with another rear support block. Place the hoses over the smaller bowls to collect the runoff from the pans. Next, plant your crops of cereal grains, such as wheat, oats, or barley. In the first pan, plant the seeds in horizontal rows. Plant the seeds in the second pan in vertical rows. Do not plant anything in the third pan. Now simulate rain by watering the three pans equally, using the same amounts of water. Observe the topsoil in the pans for the next few days. The horizontal rows duplicate the contour farming that farmers use around a hill. The vertical method, up and down a hill, prevents some soil erosion. Planting nothing at all leaves the soil unprotected. Contour farming, as in pan #1, appears to be the best way to go.

74. DIFFUSION

Molecules are the smallest parts of a substance that have the same properties as the substance itself. Molecules of gases, liquids, and solids are continuously in motion. **Diffusion** is the mixing of molecules of one substance with those of another one. Molecular motion causes diffusion.

MATERIALS: four glasses, water, sugar cube, hard candy, rock salt, dark food color, bottle of perfume or coffeepot and coffee

- Make a pot of coffee or open a bottle of perfume and observe how rapidly the aroma of coffee or perfume diffuses throughout the room.

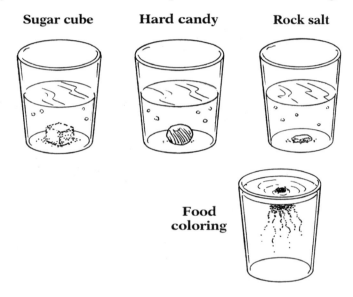

- Half-fill three glasses with water. Place the sugar cube in one, the candy in the next, and the piece of rock salt in the last one. Do not stir. Diffusion causes the dissolving (mixing) of these materials into water.

- Fill one glass nearly full. Let it stand for a few minutes. Carefully place in it one drop of a dark food color. Observe it for eight to ten minutes. Diffusion takes place due to molecular motion.

75. TESTING GROWING ROOTS FOR ACID

Knowing that acids can break apart rocks and the surface of the earth, it is interesting to realize that the roots of plants are acid.

MATERIALS: dish with glass cover, moist cotton, distilled water, several seeds, blue litmus paper

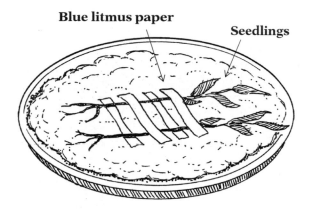

Blue litmus paper

Seedlings

- Place several seeds on the moist cotton in the dish, cover, and let the seeds germinate into small plants. When the seedlings have grown a good root system, you will be ready to run the test for acid. Moisten several strips of litmus blue with distilled water and place them over and below the rootlets. Observe over a couple of days the change in the color of the litmus blue. Make certain that the cotton is not too wet, or the test will not work.

Appendix

DENSITY OF LIQUIDS

	approx. gm/cm^3 at 20°C
Acetone	0.79
Alcohol (ethyl)	0.79
Alcohol (methyl)	0.81
Benzene	0.90
Carbon disulfide	1.29
Carbon tetrachloride	1.56
Chloroform	1.50
Ether	0.74
Gasoline	0.68
Glycerin	1.26
Kerosene	0.82
Linseed oil (boiled)	0.94
Mercury	13.6
Milk	1.03
Naphtha (petroleum)	0.67
Olive oil	0.92
Sulfuric acid	1.82
Turpentine	0.87
Water 0° C	0.99
Water 4° C	1.00
Water - sea	1.03

ALTITUDE. BAROMETER. AND BOILING POINT

altitude (approx. ft)	barometer reading (cm of mercury)	boiling point (° C)
15,430	43.1	84.9
10,320	52.0	89.8
6190	60.5	93.8
5510	62.0	94.4
5060	63.1	94.9
4500	64.4	95.4
3950	65.7	96.0
3500	66.8	96.4
3060	67.9	96.9
2400	69.6	97.6
2060	70.4	97.9
1520	71.8	98.5
970	73.3	99.0
530	74.5	99.5
0	76.0	100.0
- 550	77.5	100.5

SPECIFIC GRAVITY

gram /cm^3 at 20° C.

Agate	2.5-2.6	Granite*	2.7	Polystyrene	1.06
Aluminum	2.7	Graphite	2.2	Quartz	2.6
Brass*	8.5	Human body - normal	1.07	Rock salt	2.1-2.2
Butter	0.86	Human body - lungs full	1.00	Rubber (gum)	0.92
Cellural cellulose acetate	0.75	Ice	0.92	Silver	10.5
Celluloid	1.4	Iron (cast)*	7.9	Steel	7.8
Cement*	2.8	Lead	11.3	Sulfur (roll)	2.0
Coal (anthracite)*	1.5	Limestone	2.7	Tin	7.3
Coal (bituminous)*	1.3	Magnesium	1.74	Tungsten	18.8
Copper	8.9	Marble*	2.7	Wood Rock Elm	0.76
Cork	0.22-0.26	Nickel	8.8	Balsa	0.16
Diamond	3.1-3.5	Opal	2.1-2.3	Red Oak	0.67
German Silver	8.4	Osmium	22.5	Southern Pine	0.56
Glass (common)	2.5	Paraffin	0.9	White Pine	0.4
Gold	19.3	Platinum	21.4	Zinc	7.1

*Non homogeneous material. Specific gravity may vary. Table gives average value.

CONVERSION OF TEMPERATURE: CELSIUS TO FAHRENHEIT

C°	F°	C°	F°	C°	F°	C°	F°	C°	F°	C°	F°
250	482.00	200	392.00	150	302.00	100	212.00	50	122.00	0	32.00
249	480.20	199	390.20	149	300.20	99	210.20	49	120.20	-1	30.20
248	478.40	198	388.40	148	298.40	98	208.40	48	118.40	-2	28.40
247	476.60	197	386.60	147	296.60	97	206.60	47	116.60	-3	26.60
246	474.80	196	384.80	146	294.80	96	204.80	46	114.80	-4	24.80
245	473.00	195	383.00	145	293.00	95	203.00	45	113.00	-5	23.00
244	471.20	194	381.20	144	291.20	94	201.20	44	111.20	-6	21.20
243	469.40	193	379.40	143	289.40	93	199.40	43	109.40	-7	19.40
242	467.60	192	377.60	142	287.60	92	197.60	42	107.60	-8	17.60
241	465.80	191	375.80	141	285.80	91	195.80	41	105.80	-9	15.80
240	464.00	190	374.00	140	284.00	90	194.00	40	104.00	-10	14.00
239	462.20	189	372.20	139	282.20	89	192.20	39	102.20	-11	12.20
238	460.40	188	370.40	138	280.40	88	190.40	38	100.40	-12	10.40
237	458.60	187	368.60	137	278.60	87	188.60	37	98.60	-13	8.60
236	456.80	186	366.80	136	276.80	86	186.80	36	96.80	-14	6.80
235	455.00	185	365.00	135	275.00	85	185.00	35	95.00	-15	5.00
234	453.20	184	363.20	134	273.20	84	183.20	34	93.20	-16	3.20
233	451.40	183	361.40	133	271.40	83	181.40	33	91.40	-17	1.40
232	449.60	182	359.60	132	269.60	82	179.60	32	89.60	-18	-0.40
231	447.80	181	357.80	131	267.80	81	177.80	31	87.80	-19	-2.20
230	446.00	180	356.00	130	266.00	80	176.00	30	86.00	-20	-4.00
229	444.20	179	354.20	129	264.20	79	174.20	29	84.20	-21	-5.80
228	442.40	178	352.40	128	262.40	78	172.40	28	82.40	-22	-7.60
227	440.60	177	350.60	127	260.60	77	170.60	27	80.60	-23	-9.40
226	438.80	176	348.80	126	258.80	76	168.80	26	78.80	-24	-11.20
225	437.00	175	347.00	125	257.00	75	167.00	25	77.00	-25	-13.00
224	435.20	174	345.20	124	255.20	74	165.20	24	75.20	-26	-14.80
223	433.40	173	343.40	123	253.40	73	163.40	23	73.40	-27	-16.60
222	431.60	172	341.60	122	251.60	72	161.60	22	71.60	-28	-18.40
221	429.80	171	339.80	121	249.80	71	159.80	21	69.80	-29	-20.20
220	428.00	170	338.00	120	248.00	70	158.00	20	68.00	-30	-22.00
219	426.20	169	336.20	119	246.20	69	156.20	19	66.20	-31	-23.80
218	424.40	168	334.40	118	244.40	68	154.40	18	64.40	-32	-25.60
217	422.60	167	332.60	117	242.60	67	152.60	17	62.60	-33	-27.40
216	420.80	166	330.80	116	240.80	66	150.80	16	60.80	-34	-29.20
215	419.00	165	329.00	115	239.00	65	149.00	15	59.00	-35	-31.00
214	417.20	164	327.20	114	237.20	64	147.20	14	57.20	-36	-32.80
213	415.40	163	325.40	113	235.40	63	145.40	13	55.40	-37	-34.60
212	413.60	162	323.60	112	233.60	62	143.60	12	53.60	-38	-36.40
211	411.80	161	321.80	111	231.80	61	141.80	11	51.80	-39	-38.20
210	410.00	160	320.00	110	230.00	60	140.00	10	50.00	-40	-40.00
209	408.20	159	318.20	109	228.20	59	138.20	9	48.20	-41	-41.80
208	406.40	158	316.40	108	226.40	58	136.40	8	46.40	-42	-43.60
207	404.60	157	314.60	107	224.60	57	134.60	7	44.60	-43	-45.40
206	402.80	156	312.80	106	222.80	56	132.80	6	42.80	-44	-47.20
205	401.00	155	311.00	105	221.00	55	131.00	5	41.00	-45	-49.00
204	399.20	154	309.20	104	219.20	54	129.20	4	39.20	-46	-50.80
203	397.40	153	307.40	103	217.40	53	127.40	3	37.40	-47	-52.60
202	395.60	152	305.60	102	215.60	52	125.60	2	35.60	-48	-54.40
201	393.80	151	303.80	101	213.80	51	123.80	1	33.80	-49	-56.20

CONVERSION OF TEMPERATURE: FAHRENHEIT TO CELSIUS

F⁰	C°	F⁰	C°	F⁰	C°	F⁰	C°	F⁰	C°	F⁰	C°
250	121.11	200	93.33	150	65.56	100	37.78	50	10.00	0	-17.78
249	120.56	199	92.78	149	65.00	99	37.22	49	9.44	-1	-18.33
248	120.00	198	92.22	148	64.44	98	36.67	48	8.89	-2	-18.89
247	119.44	197	91.67	147	63.89	97	36.11	47	8.33	-3	-19.44
246	118.89	196	91.11	146	63.33	96	35.56	46	7.78	-4	-20.00
245	118.33	195	90.56	145	62.78	95	35.00	45	7.22	-5	-20.56
244	117.78	194	90.00	144	62.22	94	34.44	44	6.67	-6	-21.11
243	117.22	193	89.44	143	61.67	93	33.89	43	6.11	-7	-21.67
242	116.67	192	88.89	142	61.11	92	33.33	42	5.56	-8	-22.22
241	116.11	191	88.33	141	60.56	91	32.78	41	5.00	-9	-22.78
240	115.56	190	87.78	140	60.00	90	32.22	40	4.44	-10	-23.33
239	115.00	189	87.22	139	59.44	89	31.67	39	3.89	-11	-23.89
238	114.44	188	86.67	138	58.89	88	31.11	38	3.33	-12	-24.44
237	113.89	187	86.11	137	58.33	87	30.56	37	2.78	-13	-25.00
236	113.33	186	85.56	136	57.78	86	30.00	36	2.22	-14	-25.56
235	112.78	185	85.00	135	57.22	85	29.44	35	1.67	-15	-26.11
234	112.22	184	84.44	134	56.67	84	28.89	34	1.11	-16	-26.67
233	111.67	183	83.89	133	56.11	83	28.33	33	0.56	-17	-27.22
232	111.11	182	83.33	132	55.56	82	27.78	32	0.00	-18	-27.78
231	110.56	181	82.78	131	55.00	81	27.22	31	-0.56	-19	-28.33
230	110.00	180	82.22	130	54.44	80	26.67	30	-1.11	-20	-28.89
229	109.44	179	81.67	129	53.89	79	26.11	29	-1.67	-21	-29.44
228	108.89	178	81.11	128	53.33	78	25.56	28	-2.22	-22	-30.00
227	108.33	177	80.56	127	52.78	77	25.00	27	-2.78	-23	-30.56
226	107.78	176	80.00	126	52.22	76	24.44	26	-3.33	-24	-31.11
225	107.22	175	79.44	125	51.67	75	23.89	25	-3.89	-25	-31.67
224	106.67	174	78.89	124	51.11	74	23.33	24	-4.44	-26	-32.22
223	106.11	173	78.33	123	50.56	73	22.78	23	-5.00	-27	-32.78
222	105.56	172	77.78	122	50.00	72	22.22	22	-5.56	-28	-33.33
221	105.00	171	77.22	121	49.44	71	21.67	21	-6.11	-29	-33.89
220	104.44	170	76.67	120	48.89	70	21.11	20	-6.67	-30	-34.44
219	103.89	169	76.11	119	48.33	69	20.56	19	-7.22	-31	-35.00
218	103.33	168	75.56	118	47.78	68	20.00	18	-7.78	-32	-35.56
217	102.78	167	75.00	117	47.22	67	19.44	17	-8.33	-33	-36.11
216	102.22	166	74.44	116	46.67	66	18.89	16	-8.89	-34	-36.67
215	101.67	165	73.89	115	46.11	65	18.33	15	-9.44	-35	-37.22
214	101.11	164	73.33	114	45.56	64	17.78	14	-10.00	-36	-37.78
213	100.56	163	72.78	113	45.00	63	17.22	13	-10.56	-37	-38.33
212	100.00	162	72.22	112	44.44	62	16.67	12	-11.11	-38	-38.89
211	99.44	161	71.67	111	43.89	61	16.11	11	-11.67	-39	-39.44
210	98.89	160	71.11	110	43.33	60	15.56	10	-12.22	-40	-40.00
209	98.33	159	70.56	109	42.78	59	15.00	9	-12.78	-41	-40.56
208	97.78	158	70.00	108	42.22	58	14.44	8	-13.33	-42	-41.11
207	97.22	157	69.44	107	41.67	57	13.89	7	-13.89	-43	-41.67
206	96.67	156	68.89	106	41.11	56	13.33	6	-14.44	-44	-42.22
205	96.11	155	68.33	105	40.56	55	12.78	5	-15.00	-45	-42.78
204	95.56	154	67.78	104	40.00	54	12.22	4	-15.56	-46	-43.33
203	95.00	153	67.22	103	39.44	53	11.67	3	-16.11	-47	-43.89
202	94.44	152	66.67	102	38.89	52	11.11	2	-16.67	-48	-44.44
201	93.89	151	66.11	101	38.33	51	10.56	1	-17.22	-49	-45.00

Glossary

A

adhesion: when molecules of one kind stick to molecules of other kinds

aerobic organism: an organism that obtains its oxygen from the air

amino acids: building blocks of proteins; during digestion, proteins are broken down into these

anaerobic organism: an organism that does not need air or free oxygen

artery: blood vessel that carries blood away from the heart

asexual reproduction: reproduction requiring only one parent

atmosphere: thin layer of gases—including nitrogen, oxygen, ozone, and carbon dioxide—that surrounds the earth

auxin: hormone that regulates plant growth

B

bacteria: microorganisms found in water, air, and soil

Benedict's solution: chemical indicator used to test for sugar

bile: green liquid produced in the liver, used to emulsify fats

binary fission: a type of asexual reproduction that produces two cells of the same size

biodegradation: when materials decompose through natural means

biology: the study of living things, both plants and animals

biuret solution: chemical indicator used to test for food proteins

blood vessels: a series of tubes in the body through which blood circulates

bromthymol blue: chemical indicator used to test for acids

budding: form of asexual reproduction in which offspring forms from a bud on the parent

C

capillaries: smallest of the blood vessels

capillarity: the process by which, through a combination of cohesion and adhesion, a liquid can rise up through a solid

carbohydrate: energy-rich substance containing carbon, hydrogen, and oxygen; found in starches and sugars

carnivore: meat-eating animal or plant

casein: protein found in milk

cell: basic unit of structure of all organisms

cell division: the way new cells are produced

cell membrane: very thin outer skin of a cell

cellulose: hard material that forms the inside wall of a plant cell

chlorophyll: green material, needed for photosynthesis, found in chloroplasts

chloroplasts: the parts of a plant cell that contain chlorophyll

circulation: the moving of blood through the blood vessels that form the circulatory system

cobalt chloride: chemical indicator used to test for water

cohesion: when molecules stick to molecules of their own kind

D

deficiency disease: disease caused by lack of a vitamin or mineral in the diet

diaphragm: a muscle sheet under the lungs

diet: everything an organism eats

digestion: the process by which food is broken down for use by the body

digestive system: system of organs designed to digest food

dominant: stronger trait, in genetics

E

emulsification: keeping two liquids that do not combine with each other in suspension, one within the other

enzyme: chemical that helps food breakdown during digestion

environment: the factors and conditions that influence an organism's development

erosion: the wearing away of soil or rock by wind or water

evaporation: the conversion of a liquid by heat into vapor or steam

evaporation rate: the speed at which water evaporates

exhale: push air out

F

fat: soft, solid organic compound composed of carbon, hydrogen, and oxygen; an essential part of the human diet

fermentation: process in which yeast oxidizes sugar, producing alcohol and carbon dioxide as by-products

fertilization: when the nuclei of male and female reproductive cells join together

G

gall bladder: sac under the liver where bile is stored

gametes: reproductive cells

gastric juices: digestive fluids produced in the stomach

gene: the part of the chromosome that controls inherited traits

germination: sprouting of a seed

goiter: swelling of the thyroid gland, caused by food deficiency

gravitropism (geotropism): tendency of a plant to grow toward or away from the earth

greenhouse effect: warming of the atmosphere caused by gases reflecting heat back to the earth

H

habitat: place where a plant or animal lives

hemoglobin: iron-rich component of red blood cells

herbivore: plant-eating organism

heredity: the passing of genetic traits from parents to their offspring

homogenize: to make uniform by mixing and emulsifying

hormone: secretion that affects growth and development of an organism

hydrochloric acid: highly corrosive acid found in the digestive juices of the human stomach

hydroponics: the science of growing plants in a nutrient solution instead of in soil

I

indicator: a substance whose physical appearance changes when another specific substance is present; this change shows the presence of the second substance

indophenol: chemical indicator used to test for vitamin C

inhale: take in air

inherited traits: characteristics passed from parents to their offspring

iris: colored part of the eye that controls the amount of light entering the eye

L

lacteals: parts of the villi through which fats pass into the bloodstream

larva: second stage in the development of an insect, where the young resemble worms

limewater: chemical indicator used to test for carbon dioxide

lipase: enzyme used to break down fats

Lugol's solution: iodine-containing chemical used to test for the presence of starches

M

metamorphosis: marked change in form of an animal as it develops

minerals: substances found in nature that help the body function and develop normally

mold: simple organism of the fungus family, associated with decay; antibiotics are derived from molds

molecule: the smallest part of a substance that has the same chemical properties as the substance itself

N

nicotine: stimulant that speeds up heart rate; found in tobacco

O

offspring: new life produced by living things

organism: a living thing

osmosis: type of diffusion where liquid passes through a membrane

oxidation: the process of combining with oxygen

P

pepsin: enzyme found among the gastric juices

peristalsis: muscular movement of food along the food tube

perspiration: sweat; one of the liquid wastes of the body

photosynthesis: the food-making process in plants, using sunshine and chlorophyll

phototropism: response of a plant to light

preservative: substance added to a food to keep it from spoiling

protein: nitrogen-containing nutrient used to build and repair cells

pulse: blood spurt in the arteries

pupil: circular opening at the center of the iris

R

reactant: substance that changes during a chemical reaction

recessive: weaker trait, in genetics

red blood cell: oxygen-carrying cell in the blood

rennin: enzyme found in the gastric juices

respiration: inhalation and exhalation of air

response: an organism's reaction to a stimulus

rickets: bone deformation caused by lack of vitamin D

S

saliva: liquid that helps predigest food; found in the mouth

spore: reproductive cell

sporulation: producing new spores by the division of older spores

stethoscope: medical instrument used to listen to heartbeats

stimulus: something in the environment that causes living things to respond

stomata: small openings on the underside of plant leaves through which air passes

T

trait: characteristic of living organism

transpiration: the process through which plants emit water vapor into the atmosphere

tropism: movement of a plant toward or away from a stimulus, such as light or gravity

V

vegetative propagation: a type of asexual reproduction where one part of a plant is used to grow a new plant

villi: finger-like structures in the small intestine through which food is absorbed into the bloodstream

vitamin: nutrient that helps the body regulate growth and development

W

white blood cell: blood cell that helps fight infection

Y

yeast: single-celled microscopic plant

Index

A

adhesion, 20
aerobic organisms, 5
anaerobic organisms, 5
anemia, 30
aphids, infestation by, 42
asexual reproduction
    budding, 46
    sporulation, 47
    vegetative propagation, 47
asthma, 44
auxin, 2

B

beetles, 55
Benedict's solution, 22
beriberi, 29
bile, 37
biodegradation, 28
biological control, 43
biuret solution, 25
bromthymol blue, 7
budding, 9, 46

C

calcium, 30
capillaries, 38
capillarity, 20
carbon dioxide, 6, 7, 8, 9, 10, 11, 17, 18
casein, 35
castings, 54
cell
    membrane, 21
    model, gelatin, 21
chemical indicator, 6
chemotropism, 2
chlorophyll, 27
chloroplasts, 27
chromatography, 27

circulation
    animal, 19
    plant, 20
Clinitest sugar test, 22
clotting, 29
cobalt chloride paper, 12
cohesion, 20
colloid solution, 42
comfort index, 45
cytoplasm, 21

D

diffusion, 62
digestion, 32–37
    chemical, 32, 33
    heat, in, 36
    mechanical, 32

E

earthworms, 53–54
emphysema, 44
emulsification, 37
environment, 51
    and gene influence, 50
enzymes, 32, 33
erosion, 60
evaporation rate, 16

F

fats, 23, 37
fermentation, 46
fish, and color, 51
Francesco, 45
fruit flies, 48–49

G

gastric juices, 34–35
genes, 50
geotropism, 2

germination, 48
goiter, 30
gravitropism, 2
greenhouse effect, 10

H

habitat, 52
heartbeat, 39–40
heliotropism, 2
homogenization, 37
hydrochloric acid, 34–35
hydroponics, 58–59
hydrotropism, 2

I

indicator, chemical, 6
indophenol, 26
insect multiplication, 48–49
iodine, 30
iron, 30, 31

L

lacteals, 38
limewater, 6–8, 17
lipase, 37
Lugol's solution, 21

M

metamorphosis, 55
microweather. *See* transpiration.
minerals
    deficiency, 30
    nutritional, summary, 30
    testing for, 23
mold, 47
molecules, 62

N

nicotine, 41, 42
night blindness, 29
nucleus, 21

O

organisms, anaerobic, 5
osmosis, 38
oxidation, 6, 45
oxygen, 5, 6, 7, 10, 17, 18

P

pepsin, 35
peristalsis, 31
pest control, 43
phosphorus, 30
photosynthesis, 8, 18, 27
phototropism, 2
potassium, 30
protein, 24, 38
pulse, 39, 40

R

Redi, Francesco, 45
Redi's experiment, 45
relative temperature, 45
rennin, 34, 35
respiration, 8
response, 1
rickets, 29

S

saliva, 32
scurvy, 26
sexual reproduction
    germination, 48
sodium, 30
soil erosion, 60
solution, colloid, 42
sounds, 56
spores, 47, 60
sporulation, 47
starch, 21
stimulus, 1
stomata, 11, 12
sugar, testing for, 22

T

temperature, relative, 45
testing for
    carbon dioxide, 8
    fats, 23
    minerals, 23
    protein, 24
    starch, 21
    sugar, 22
    vitamin C, 26
    water in food, 26
    water presence, 12
thigmotropism, 2

traits, inherited, 50
transpiration, 12
tuber, 47

V

vegetative propagation, 47
villi, 38
vitamin C, 26
vitamins, 29

W

water, testing for, 26
water evaporation. *See* transpiration.
weathering, 60
wormery, 53
worms, 52–55

Y

yeast, 9, 46

Z

zinc, 30